CHOSEN!
WON!

Copyright © 2007 Concordia Publishing House
3558 S. Jefferson Avenue
St. Louis, MO 63118-3968
1-800-325-3040 • www.cph.org

Library of Congress Cataloging-in-Publication Data
Chosen! won! : devotions for teens by teens.
    p. cm.
  ISBN 978-0-7586-1111-6
  1. Christian teenagers--Prayers and devotions. I. Concordia
Publishing House.

  BV4850.C52 2007
  242'.63--dc22   2007000987

1 2 3 4 5 6 7 8 9 10   16 15 14 13 12 11 10 09 08 07

devotions

CHOSEN!
WON!

+CHOSEN+

for teens by teens

CONCORDIA PUBLISHING HOUSE · SAINT LOUIS

Our thanks to our teen authors:

Stephanie Allman
Johanna Beldon
Samantha Berard
Jewelle Bickel
Rich Bimler
Kendra Borglum
Shannon Burthold
Bo Cappelli
Joshua Dehnke
Erica Demel
Sarah DeMuth
Rebecca Difatta

Erin Dittmer
Terry Dittmer
Ross Engel
Doug Fiehler
Donine Fink
Broderick Gerald
Elisabeth Gulliford
Andy Harrigan
Jenny Harris
T. J. Hoffman
Aaron Hosmon
Heather Huss
Kathleen Joza
Hillary Kneubuhl

Stacy Kolb
Stephen Kreher
Steven T. Lessner
Hannah Long
Amanda Luedtke
Jason Marcus
Katie Maske
Brittany McIntyre
Cameron McMasters
Kara Miller
Nichole Mueller
Christine Oberdeck
Philip J. Potyondy
Jamie Poyak
Tom Roma

Heather Scheiwe
Janelle Schmitt
Barbara Short
Jeffrey Teeple
Sarah Trinklein
Kelsey Wagner
Sarah Wahnefried
Carolyn Walsh
Kelly Warneke
Jenna Whitaker
Lisa Widlowski
Rebecca Wiechman
Julie Willbrand
Erin Winters
Amy Wood

CHOSEN! WON!

But you are a chosen people, a royal priesthood, a holy nation, a people belonging to God, that you may declare the praises of Him who called you out of darkness into His wonderful light.

—1 Peter 2:9—

The summer of 2007 marked thirty years since the very first LCMS National Youth Gathering. This triennial event brings together thousands of young people from across the United States. They come to celebrate their lives as God's children, His chosen ones, who were won at the cross through the suffering, death, and resurrection of their Savior, Jesus.

This collection of sixty devotions written for teens by teens celebrates this milestone event. Some of the authors are teens today, while others were teens who attended the very first Gathering. Many of those early writers have gone on to lead youth who attended later Gatherings. While our authors may be separated by nearly a generation, their messages still speak to the lives of teens today.

CHOSEN IN CHRIST

They will make war against the Lamb, but the Lamb will overcome them because He is Lord of lords and King of kings— and with Him will be His called, chosen, and faithful followers.

—Revelation 17:14—

MARTHA, MARTHA, MARTHA

Things to Do: Finish reading *The Scarlet Letter* for American Literature. E-mail Coach Frank about missing basketball practice on Friday. Help address envelopes for missions offering mailing at church. Read my Bible. Write paper about Crusades for history class. Take Luke out for ice cream . . . sibling bonding time! Do Algebra homework—p. 102–103 #5–72. Go out for coffee with Kelsey. Go for a run! Do my chores.

Does your list of things to do—either written or mental—ever look like this? Filled with homework, tasks, activities, time with friends and family . . . and time with God stuck in there where it fits? I know that, at times, mine sure does. I know that I'm busy, but it's hard for me to decide what I should cut out of my life—it all seems like good

Read: Luke 10:38–42

stuff! I can come up with valid reasons to do everything on my list, and to be involved in everything I have in my life. There's nothing wrong with helping out at my church, hanging out with friends, playing sports, and doing homework, but sometimes, when I do all that, it seems like there's barely any time to spend with God.

Often, I feel like I imagine Martha must have felt when Jesus came to visit her house—and probably throughout the rest of her daily life as well! She got caught up in "all the preparations that had to be made" (Luke 10:40). This probably meant cleaning up her house and making food for Jesus and His disciples. In other words, doing things for Him because she thought she was serving Him! There's nothing wrong with any of these things in themselves. As much as you'd like to tell your mom this when it's your turn to clean the bathroom, doing chores is not a sin!

If you continue reading Luke's account, however, Martha's problem becomes evident. She was spending time *doing* things instead of simply being with Jesus! Here she was with the Savior of the entire world in her living room, and she was off in the kitchen doing stuff! To top it off, she got upset that her sister wasn't helping her. Martha approaches Jesus about it, expecting Him to take her side. Instead, He agreed with Mary's actions, saying, "Mary has chosen what is better" (Luke 10:42). There's nothing wrong with serving others, and with fulfilling the duties that God has placed in our lives— being a student, a family member, a friend. The problem comes when our lives are so filled up with those things that we aren't spending time at the feet of Jesus.

I don't know about you, but it's hard to cut things out of my life so that I have more time with God. Our human nature wants to do stuff, and thinks that, the more we do, the more God will like us! Like Martha, sometimes it's easy to feel like our lives are made of the things we do—our successes and achievements—and our identity is sometimes found in the activities we participate in. How far is that from the truth, though! Our identities are really in Christ, and Him alone! He doesn't want us to run ourselves ragged doing things to make Him like us more. He already loves us enough that He died for us! He wants us to serve Him, but He also wants to spend time with us. He wants us to sit at His feet (figuratively speaking) like Mary did, so that we can learn from Him in His Word and grow in our relationship with Him. It is at these moments, sitting at His feet, when we are still, that we can really "know that [He] is God" (Psalm 46:1).

Pray: Dear Lord Jesus, thank You for the identity that You've given me that is found not in what I do but in You. Thank You for dying on the cross for me, so that I don't have to earn my way into Your favor by my acts of service or my activities. Please help me prioritize my time so that I can spend time at Your feet. Show me the things in my life that I need to change or eliminate, so that my schedule glorifies You, and so that I am not so distracted by everything I do that I forget about what's really important—You! In Your name I pray. Amen.

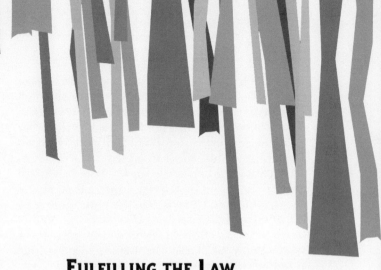

FULFILLING THE LAW

In our society, we do something to get something. Listen to the television, radio, books, magazines, and fill your life with conditional promises. "Take this pill, *then* you will lose weight." "Use this lotion and you *will* be better looking." "Shop at this store . . . Eat this food . . . Believe in this man . . . Do—*and you will have everything you want or need.*"

We want to be in charge. Even in the first century, people lived this life. "Now a man came up to Jesus and asked, 'Teacher, what good thing must I do to get eternal life?'" (Matthew 19:16). You do something to get something. Makes sense, doesn't it? "How many times do I *have* to go to church?" "Is it necessary to read the Bible *every day*?" "Lord, how many times shall I forgive my brother when he sins against me?" (Matthew 18:21).

Jesus replied, "'If you want to enter life, obey the commandments'" (Matthew 19:17). *Don't* mur-

Read: Matthew 19:16–26

der, lie, steal; *do* honor your parents and love your neighbor (Matthew 18–19). Jesus pointed that rich young ruler and all of us to the Ten Commandments because we asked Him to. Jesus says to us, "Okay, you want to do something, try these ten." God gives us our "to do" list. God chimes in with one more stipulation, "You must keep this law perfectly, or else, you will die."

"'All these I have kept,' the young man said. 'What do I still lack?' Jesus answered, 'If you want to be perfect, go, sell your possessions and give to the poor, and you will have treasure in heaven. Then come, follow Me'" (Matthew 19:20–21).

We look at our top ten list and feel pretty satisfied with the way we are living. However, He asks us to do the things we cannot do or do not want to do, and like the man, we go away sad.

The rich young man couldn't do it; he couldn't be perfect. We can't do it either. If we can't "do something," then how will we "get something"? "[The disciples] were greatly astonished and asked, 'Who then can be saved?'" (Matthew 19:25).

We humbly come to God with our failures, and He directs our eyes to perfection personified. "This is how God showed His love among us: He sent His one and only Son into the world that we might live through Him. This is love: not that we loved God, but that He loved us and sent His Son as an atoning sacrifice for our sins" (1 John 4:9–10). "Therefore love is the fulfillment of the Law" (Romans 13:10). Jesus took our sins and poured out His life on the cross for us, so that we might live eternally. Here it is in our language: We sin, so we die. The perfect Lamb dies for us, so we live. "With man this is impossible, but with God all things are possible" (Matthew 19:26).

Pray: Dear heavenly Father, I come to You in humility. I have tried to win salvation on my own and have ignored You. Forgive me for my pride. Lord, thank You for the amazing gift of Your only Son, who bore the cross for me. Help me to live a life of thanksgiving and love. In Your most precious name. Amen.

CHOSEN OUT OF THE WORLD

Being Happy in an Unhappy World. The Tao of Inner Peace. Contentment: The Way to True Happiness. Books like these abound in bookstores, at online stores, and on their readers' bookshelves. They promise all kinds of answers and solutions to the problems presented by the crazy, mixed-up world in which we live. And it's no wonder—people seek happiness like pirates hunted buried treasure! In this world, happiness *is* a treasure, rare and hard to come by. The media seems to scream at people, "Don't be content! Want more! Get more! You deserve it!" Just turn on the television and you'll see all kinds of examples of this world's pollutants. Murders, drugs, kidnappings . . . the list doesn't end. All of these sad happenings stem from sin, and all

Read: John 15:19

leave people feeling disheartened and unhappy.

As Christians, though, we know whom to turn to in the face of so much adversity and hardship. Instead of self-help books, we can peruse the one book that truly has answers for us, in the form of God's very words—the Bible. There we see an immeasurable amount of comfort in the hope we have in Him! There He tells us He has something better for us than this world and its sorry state. We no longer have to be affiliated with it; just because we are in this world at this moment does not mean we are *of* it.

Jesus says He chose us out of the world, meaning that we are no longer a part of it. We are separated, detached, disjointed. What a comfort that knowledge is, especially when the weight of the world is so smothering and things seem utterly hopeless! "I have come that they may have life," Jesus said, "and have it to the full" (John 10:10). Those words make me feel so appreciated, so loved. God chose me and wants me to have life—a full, rich one at that. So that I may have that full life, He has separated me from this sorry world, and I'm inexpressibly thankful.

Pray: Dear Jesus, sometimes the things of this world just seem like too much for me to handle! Everything bears down on me and I just feel so helpless, so overwhelmed. Help me to remember that You've separated me from this world. You have a great plan for me, that I may have life "to the full"! Thank You so much for that and for all You do for me, Lord. Amen.

LIFE'S FINAL

How do you feel when you think about the end of something? Depends what's ending, right? In Matthew 24, Jesus tells His disciples that the end is coming and goes on to describe signs that point to the end of the world. Is the end of the world a good thing or a bad thing?

Jesus uses some pretty scary imagery to explain the signs of the end. Look again at the words He uses. That doesn't sound like a good thing! In fact, it's pretty depressing. Kind of like the verses from Isaiah that say, "The grass withers and the flowers fall, because the breath of the Lord blows on them. Surely the people are grass. The grass withers and the flowers fall, but the Word of our God stands forever" (40:7–8).

Great, so we're all going to pass away, and we're like *dead grass!* Well that sounds like an excellent ending, doesn't it? But look closer at what Jesus is really telling us. Both Isaiah's and Matthew's descriptions of the end conclude with a promise. Isaiah's passage ends, "but the Word of our God stands forever" (40:8). In Matthew's Gospel Jesus says, "but My words

 Read: Matthew 24:23–28, 34–35

will never pass away" (24:35). These statements hold a powerful, comforting promise for us.

Let's consider another end—the end of a school year. The last business of the year is finals. Our death, or the end of the world, is like life's final. Wake up! See the signs! The final is coming, and what's worse, we don't know when. But most people find that a final isn't so bad if they know the material, and God left us a study guide. It's more than a study guide, really, it's an answer sheet.

The Bible is the answer sheet for life's final. And it gets even better! There is only one question—*How am I saved?* The answer? *JESUS!* The final is multiple choice, so don't be tricked by wrong answers. If you pick, "I'll be saved because I'm a good person," you'll fail the final. If you pick, "All I need is my stuff and all the fun I've had," you'll fail the final. If you pick, "I don't know, I've never really thought about it," you'll fail the final.

As humans, we'll pick the wrong choices every time. That's why there's even more good news. Through the Word the Holy Spirit gives us the right answer, and we believe it! Jesus died to take away all of your wrong choices and He lives to be the right answer. So as you live from day to day, don't forget that someday the time will come for life's final. And hang out with Jesus along the way, because He's a great friend who's taken the greatest final, the cross, for you.

Pray: Dear Lord, sometimes I am scared of the future. Life can be so uncertain and stressful. Forgive me for not trusting in You with all of my hopes and dreams. Help me to remember that You are in control of everything. Thank You for providing me with the final answer that I need through Jesus' death and resurrection. In the name of my only hope and salvation, Jesus Christ. Amen.

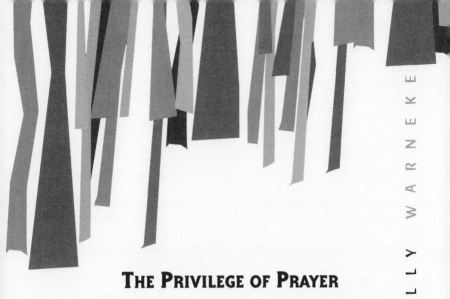

THE PRIVILEGE OF PRAYER

If you could spend ten minutes with anyone in the world, who would it be? Your favorite movie star? The President of the United States? The lead singer of your favorite band? Imagine that person actually offered to give you ten minutes of their time . . . ten minutes to talk with them about whatever you want, and they'd listen to your every word. What are the chances that you'd blow them off and tell them, "I'm too busy" or "I just don't want to talk to you"? Probably pretty slim, right?

Now, imagine that God, the Creator of the universe, the most supreme Being, the Savior of the entire world, actually offered to give you not only ten minutes of His time, but every moment of every day to talk to Him. Imagine that He said to you, "I'm here, ready to listen to you whenever you want! You can approach Me with confidence!" Does it make a whole lot of sense to blow Him off, saying,

Read: Hebrews 4:16; Philippians 4:6–7

"I'm too busy" or "I just don't want to talk to You"?

Well, in case you haven't figured it out by now . . . God has told us just that. Hebrews 4:16 tells us that we can "approach the throne of grace with confidence," and Philippians 4:6 says that "in everything, by prayer and petition, with thanksgiving," we can "present [our] requests to God."

What a privilege we have! Sometimes I feel like I have to pray, like it's something that I have to do because I'm a Christian, and that if I don't pray every day, I'm not doing such a great job. When I think about it not as a command but like meeting with someone famous, I realize what an honor this is—to be able to spend time talking to someone—not just a movie star or the president, but God! That's when I remember that the reason I pray is not because it makes me a great Christian . . . but because instead of being obligated, I have the privilege of praying, because of God's great grace and love for me!

In prayer, we can approach God with anything—our hopes and fears, our concerns and problems, our tough decisions, our friends' and family's requests, our thanks and praises. God might not always respond to these things in the way that we, in our human understanding, want Him to respond. We do know, however, that whatever His answer, His will is ultimately always accomplished, and that He is working for the ultimate good of His kingdom (see Romans 8:28).

So as you go about your life—today and this week and this month and this year—remember the great privilege that you have. You can approach God, the Creator of the universe, the Savior of the world, with your prayers!

Pray: Dear Lord, thank You so much for the incredible privilege that You have given me—to approach You in prayer, not with fear, but with confidence! Teach me how You want me to pray, and help me speak to You daily in prayer—not because I'm obligated to, but because I want to! In Your name I pray. Amen.

SAMANTHA BERARD

ME! CHOSEN?

Have you ever been the unlucky one chosen to read something out loud in class when you didn't want to? Maybe you were chosen to do some task that seemed impossible. If your life is like mine, I know that you have. When this happens to me, I sometimes just want to put it down, forget about it, and give up.

Then I remember that Jesus was chosen to do what was an impossible task for you and me—to live a perfect life, to die on the cross, and rise again in order to take away all of our sins. He didn't really have much of a say in it either. His heavenly Father chose Him. Jesus was obedient to the Father's will and did what He demanded. Jesus could have given up at any time. When it got too hard, He could have said, "That's it" or "I'm done." Thank God He did-n't—literally.

The next time you are chosen to do that

Read: Psalm 18:18–19

awful oral report in front of the class that you are dreading or have to stick up for what you believe in, tell yourself not to quit. You can turn to the strength God gives you in His Word.

Just as the Father did not leave Jesus to face His challenges alone so He does not leave us to face life's challenges on our own. God gives us the promise of continued care through His Word and Sacraments. We can face all our life's challenges because Christ faced our greatest challenge for us.

Pray: Heavenly Father, help us not to get discouraged and lose faith in You when we are faced with a challenge we were chosen to do. Give us the strength and support that we need to accomplish our goals. In Jesus' name I pray. Amen.

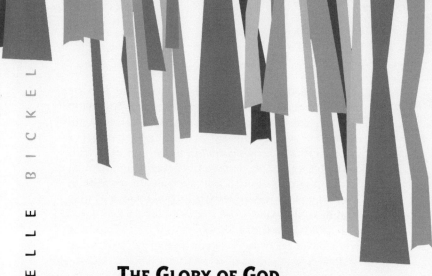

THE GLORY OF GOD

Sometimes amidst difficult times, I become a bit skeptical about God and what He is doing. I look at my life, and all I can see is painful experiences. It is during these same times that I feel that the Lord is really directing that question at me. He is in a sense saying, "Hello, did you not hear what I said? If you believe, you will see God's splendor."

This past year has been full of disappointment for me. I have had some great friendships go down the drain. I have been the one who has not made the team. It seems at times like just a big pile-up of trials, leaving me struggling to hold on. During this time, I am flooded by heaps of doubts. I feel devastated, like I was sent back to square one. There lie these thoughts: How often have I questioned God's will for my life and thought that I could do so much better? How many times have I placed God in a box saying that in a sense He could

Read: John 11:40

never achieve the impossible?

At times like these I can turn to God's Word and see His promises to me, promises so wonderful that they are beyond my human understanding, a promise that sent His own Son to die and rise again, so that I might live with Him forever. Then, to calm my fears and quiet my uncertainties, the Lord answers me, "My glory will be revealed to you, you can trust and believe in Me."

When you go through painful times, doubting your Savior really can't get you anywhere, except possibly, leading to more worry and more fear. As we grow in our faith, the Holy Spirit guides us to trust in Him, to open our eyes to His will in our lives.

Pray: Dear Lord, help me to accept Your will for my life and truly trust and believe in Your almighty power. Amen.

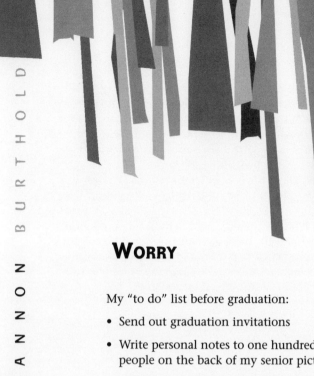

WORRY

My "to do" list before graduation:

- Send out graduation invitations

- Write personal notes to one hundred or so people on the back of my senior pictures

- Update all my photo albums/scrapbooks

- Tour college campuses

- Figure out what I'm going to do for the rest of my life so I can pick a major and register for classes

- Write a bunch of scholarship essays so I can afford to go to college

- Maintain a 25–35 hour work week so I can save money to go to Spain

- Buy a car to get myself to college

Read: Matthew 6:25

I sit here worrying about how in the world all of this is possibly going to get done. I worry that I will make the wrong decision when choosing my major, and all the people I will disappoint if I don't make it in the world as I plan. I then remember that I'm not perfect, and that God will take me in no matter how many people I disappoint in my lifetime.

God doesn't want us to worry about our life like so many of us do, including myself. I need to remind myself that none of the things listed above will help me get to heaven, and that Jesus Christ has taken care of that for me already through His suffering, death, and resurrection. Through His gift of faith He provides all that I need in this life and the next.

Pray: Dear Lord, remind me not to worry about my life and the things I stress over. Help me remember that this all will be of no importance when it is time for us to enter Your kingdom. In Your name I pray. Amen.

STEPHEN KREHER

LETTING GOD'S PEACE RULE

We have all had to make decisions that affect the course of our life. Now more than ever we, as teenagers, are making choices that will forever shape our life. Some of those decisions come easily, and others leave you confused and without direction. But there is direction. It may not come overnight or the next day, but when it does, you will feel a peace in your heart that only comes from God.

Now more than ever I have had to find God's will as I study His Word and seek the peace for my heart that only He can give. Senior year means I will be graduating from high school and leaving for college. There are many uncertainties that come with senior year. These uncertainties include what college to go to, what to major in, and especially what to do with my life. Many times I have to stop and ask myself about a certain situation, "Do I have

Read: Colossians 3:15

peace in my heart?" I am glad I have God's direction in my life, because I would feel lost without it.

When we trust God to lead us, He gives us peace within. As you seek God's will, you'll not only feel peaceful, but satisfied and filled with joy. God's Spirit guides us in our decisions as we study His Word and come to God in prayer.

As Christ's chosen people, we are given His direction and peace that comes with following His will. Jesus left us with a great gift called peace (John 14:27), and that is to help us know the will of God when making decisions. When you feel God's peace, go for it! If you don't, then wait until peace comes. Let the peace that only Christ can give rule in your heart!

Pray: Dear God, thank You for sending Your Son to live and to die for us, and especially for choosing us to receive Your gift of peace. It's only through You that we may have direction and peace within. Amen.

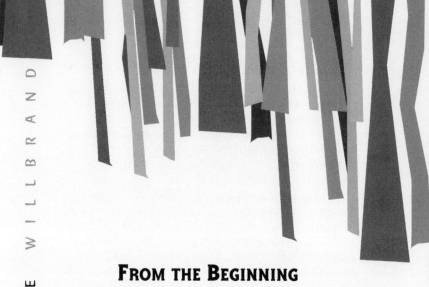

JULIE WILLBRAND

FROM THE BEGINNING

From. The. Beginning. Those three little words from Paul's second letter to the Thessalonians are seemingly insignificant at first glance, but when you stop to consider their context, the value within becomes more apparent. God was sending the people of Thessalonica a very important message, one that still encourages us today!

Paul's stay in the huge city of Thessalonica was brief. However, he still had much left to teach the people there—so he wrote to them. In his first letter, Paul had said, "May He strengthen your hearts so that you will be blameless and holy in the presence of our God and Father when our Lord Jesus comes" (1 Thessalonians 3:13), which was a bit confusing. The Thessalonians began to feel disillusioned; how could they ever be blameless and holy in God's presence? In his second letter, Paul assured them using the words from today's reading. They

Read: 2 Thessalonians 2:13–14

were absolutely correct—they *couldn't* measure up to God's standards on their own. However, God had chosen them *from the very beginning*. He chose them to be saved! Through Jesus' sacrifice, they were washed clean. When they would appear blameless in the sight of God, it would be because Jesus' immaculate image made them pure, not because of their actions.

Just as the Thessalonians wondered long ago about how they would ever measure up to God's standards, we still question today. We do it in different ways and toward different subjects, but it all boils down to the same question: "How can I ever be good enough?" Like Paul's answer to the Thessalonians, our answer is the same: We can't be good enough, but Jesus can. He chose us from the very beginning—before we were even conceived, before our parents were born, before even our farthest known relatives lived and breathed—before all that, our names were written in God's Book of Life. Picture that, God writing your name on a clean, white page. He knew your name; He knew everything about you. Most importantly, He chose you, so you would not have to do the impossible. What a weight that lifts from our shoulders! In response to His invaluable gift, we can share the Gospel with those around us, that they too "might share in the glory of our Lord Jesus Christ" (2 Thessalonians 2:14).

So, the next time you're feeling inadequate, unappreciated, or disillusioned, remember that way back in history (circa AD 52), the people of Thessalonica were feeling exactly the same way. However, Paul had a message from God for them that God also wants you to understand: He chose you and sent His Son to save you from your imperfection. That's all there is to it. You don't need to measure up, because Christ did everything for you.

Pray: God, thank You so much for choosing me—I know I could never measure up on my own. Help me to share Your love with those around me, so that they too may come to have a relationship with You. You are amazing, God! Amen.

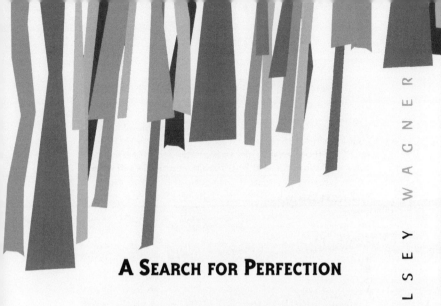

A SEARCH FOR PERFECTION

A perfectionist is someone who expects everything to be perfect. They set extremely high standards and become upset when those standards aren't met. You can probably picture someone like that right now—someone who carefully plans and executes every little detail of their job, someone who won't rest until everything fits their perfect standards. You could be thinking of a sibling, teacher, friend, or maybe even yourself.

Unfortunately, no matter how hard we try, the search for perfection is meaningless. As long as there is sin in the world, no one can ever be truly perfect. While we try to achieve perfection on earth, we stand before God as sinful failures. The Thessalonians were bothered by this. They thought that in order to be saved they had to be completely holy and blameless before God, something that no one can achieve on their own. Paul wrote a letter to the Thessalonians to correct and encourage them.

 Read: 2 Thessalonians 2:13–17

What Paul wrote to the church in Thessalonica still applies to us today. We cannot achieve forgiveness and salvation through our own power. We can never be holy before God without help. The only way we can be perfect and holy before God is through faith in His Son. We were lost in our sins so God chose to sacrifice His only Son, so that we could be forgiven.

In our efforts to live a holy, God-pleasing life, we always sin and come up short. Jesus Christ lived the perfect life for us. He was sinless, He resisted all temptation, and He was able to put God before everything. Through Jesus' death and resurrection we are able to stand before God perfect, holy, and blameless. God has chosen us to receive this perfection. Before we were born, before time began, before God created the world, we were chosen to receive this gift of salvation and eternal life through faith in Jesus Christ. We have also been chosen by God to share this gift with all people. We are called to be God's witnesses. Our words and actions show our faith to those around us.

The gift of salvation we receive from Christ is more important than any task we want to accomplish on earth. So the next time you see someone struggling to achieve perfection, remind them that true perfection is found only through faith in Christ Jesus.

Pray: Dear Lord, even though we don't like to admit it, we know that we are not perfect. We try hard, but we always fall short of the plans You have for us, and we ask for Your forgiveness. Thank You for sending Your Son as a sacrifice, so that we may be forgiven and receive the gift of salvation. Help us to share this gift with others. In Your name we pray. Amen.

A NEW FAMILY

Baptism is our birth into new life, a life filled with the love of our Father. A new family is ours, for we are now children of God. It doesn't matter what age you are in this life. When you get baptized, you are only a child in God's eyes. In the family of Christ, you age not by how many years you have lived, but by how God knows you. He is your Father. He gives us rules to live by in His Commandments. He gives us His love and care. He even gave us His only Son, Jesus, to die for our sins. What a wonderful Father! This new family we belong to is filled with love, joy, and honesty. This family will last for all of eternity.

God our Father will not abandon us as orphans; He will come to us. He lives with us and in us. He teaches us what we need to know to prepare for the future.

The apostle Paul uses adoption to illustrate

 Read: John 14:18

the believer's new relationship with God. In Roman culture, the adopted person lost all rights in his old family and gained all the rights of a legitimate child in his new family. He became a full heir to his father's estate. Likewise, when a person becomes a Christian, he or she gains all the privileges and responsibilities of a child in God's family. One of these outstanding privileges is being led by the Holy Spirit (see Galatians 4:5–6).

Pray: Dear Father, thank You for adopting us into Your family. Help me to spread Your Word and wisdom to everyone I see. Let me know I can call on You in my time of need, and remind me of that even when things are going right. You are the best Father anyone could ask for. Amen.

REBECCA WIECHMAN

GOD DID IT!

The biology teacher stood in front of the class and pointed at a chart. At one end of the chart was an ape with long swinging arms, and at the other end, a hairy kind of stooped-over man. The teacher smiled and said, "This is how man evolved."

One boy, a little confused and fearful, shot his hand in the air and said, "But I believe in the Bible." The class waited silently, but the teacher quickly dismissed the comment and continued, "This is how we . . ."

The boy raised his hand, more timidly this time, and said quietly, "God made Adam, the first man, right?" The teacher paid no attention at all.

This situation occurs many times in schools across the country. How do we reconcile what we read in Genesis with what we hear in science class? How do Adam and Eve fit with an anthropologist's idea of the "first man"?

Read: Genesis 1–3

The world constantly tries to say the story of creation is made up. But as Christians we remember God did it! We are definitely not here by accident, nor are we here to merely please ourselves during our short stay on earth. We owe our existence to God. Every atom of hydrogen, every star in the sky, and every blade of grass is here because God wants it to be. In Genesis, God, the artist, signs His picture saying, "This is Mine."

God pays us a high compliment in Genesis. After making everything else, God made man. In fact, He made man in His own image, holy and blameless. When He was finished with all of creation, God commented to Himself, "Very good." He even put Adam in charge of His creation. He was obviously satisfied, and no one except God has ever been completely satisfied with man since then!

We were made good and perfect, but temptation and sin lurked just around the corner. We have lived with the consequences of sin ever since, but, thankfully, we don't have to live with the punishment. God promised Adam and Eve, and us, forgiveness and salvation in His own Son.

The next time you learn about evolution, just remember, "God did it!" State your case, and if the teacher disagrees, just remember—you are not the descendant of an ape but rather of a perfect God.

Pray: Lord, help me through the times my faith in You is put to the test. Help me remember You did it—You created the whole universe. Give me the courage to share this fact with people who don't know it. In Jesus' name. Amen.

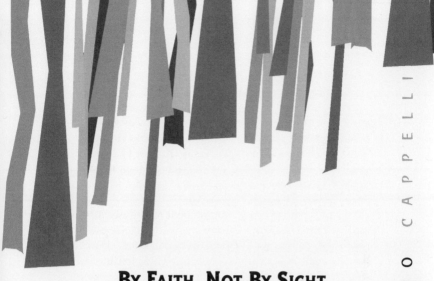

BY FAITH, NOT BY SIGHT

It was electrifying news—Jesus Christ had risen from the dead, just as He said He would! "We have seen the Lord," some of the disciples cried. But Thomas couldn't bring himself to believe it. "Unless I see the nail marks in His hands and put my finger where the nails were, and put my hand into His side. I will not believe it" (John 20:25).

Thomas's doubt evaporated a week later when he saw the resurrected Christ face-to-face and examined His wounds. Then Jesus told him, "Because you have seen Me, you have believed; blessed are those who have not seen and yet have believed" (John 20:29).

"Those who have not seen and yet have believed." That describes you and me. We have been called to worship the invisible God. Our faith does not rest on physical signs or manifestations. Our beliefs sometimes go contrary to what logic and

Read: 2 Corinthians 4:15; 5:7

physical sense indicate. Faith is "being sure of what we hope for and certain of what we do not see" (Hebrews 11:1).

"So," Paul wrote, "we fix our eyes not on what is seen, but on what is unseen. For what is seen is temporary, but what is unseen is eternal. . . . We live by faith, not by sight" (2 Corinthians 4:18; 5:7).

I have no idea what the future holds in store for me or for you. We walk through life trusting in Jesus, our Shepherd, to lead us safely. Our path at times will wind through green pastures and beside still waters. At other times it may traverse the valley of the shadow of death. But God is with us today as He was with His people long ago.

As Christians, we have the advantage of knowing that the steps we take in faith lead to a definite and positive goal. Peter explains this comforting truth when he writes, "Though you have not seen Him, you love Him; and even though you do not see Him now, you believe in Him and are filled with an inexpressible and glorious joy, for you are receiving the goal of your faith, the salvation of your souls" (1 Peter 1:8–9).

Pray: Father, I can't see You, but I know with certainty that You are with me and that You loved me enough to send Your only Son to the cross for me. Give me Your Holy Spirit's help to cling to that certainty always. Amen.

IT'S BY MY SPIRIT

ELISABETH GULLIFORD

My little brother John was born with Down Syndrome. My family had a difficult time adjusting to that fact right after he was born. How would John get along when he wouldn't be able to do all the things that other kids his age could do?

One night we read a verse from the Old Testament. "This is the Word of the Lord. . . . Not by might nor by power, but by My Spirit, says the Lord Almighty" (Zechariah 4:6). In a vision, God told His prophet Zechariah to depend not on might or power, but on His Holy Spirit.

John will never have all the "might and power" that other kids his age have, but that's okay. Nothing we have in life depends on our own might and power. We're proud of John for his own efforts. And, more importantly, we know Jesus loves him.

God shows us over and over in His Word that our own power and might accomplishes little.

 Read: Zechariah 4:6

Gideon thought he needed a huge army to defeat the Midianites. But God sent men away until there were only three hundred soldiers in Gideon's army. That victory was the Lord's, won with His might and power. Joshua, too, knew who would win the battle of Jericho when he marched his people around the city seven times and then commanded, "Shout! For the Lord has given you the city!" (Joshua 6:16).

It is tempting to accept all the praise for ourselves when we feel we have accomplished something great. In those times, along with feeling good about what we have accomplished, we thank God for the power and might His Holy Spirit put in us at our Baptism. It is God's power in us that helps us accomplish things and, best of all, helps us believe in Jesus' victory on the cross.

Pray: Jesus, remind me that I don't have to accomplish everything with my own talent and strength. Fill me with Your power and might that I might, in Your grace, accomplish all You set before me. Amen.

CELEBRATE LIFE

Nobody likes me. I'm not pretty enough or smart enough or clever enough. I'm never going to school again.

Have you ever felt that way? I have—a lot lately. What do I do? How do I get up in the morning? I remember some of the things that have happened in my life and what God taught me through them.

I was only three weeks old when God saved me from death. I was born with a cleft palate—an opening in the roof of my mouth. The young interns who examined me at birth didn't even notice it. The cleft palate caused feeding problems and made me lose so much weight that my parents rushed me to the hospital on Christmas Day. Those same two doctors were in the emergency room, fighting to save my life.

God has a plan for each of us, even as we

Read: Psalm 139

grow in our mother's womb (Psalm 139:13–16). God used those doctors that day to keep His purpose for me alive.

Last year I had major surgery on my back. God taught me a lot as I lay in the hospital. The nurses understood what I was going through and helped me through the rough times. My classmates and friends and family kept me in their prayers. Through their cards and phone calls and visits they reminded me that I was in their thoughts and that God was still in control of my life. If I can live through a five-hour surgery and be back on my feet in less than a week, God can help me face anything with His courage and strength.

You are special. God had a plan for you before you were even born. Paul tells us, "For while we are in this tent [earthly body], we groan and are burdened, because we do not wish to be unclothed but to be clothed with our heavenly dwelling, so that what is mortal may be swallowed up by life. Now it is God who has made us for this very purpose and has given us the Spirit as a deposit, guaranteeing what is to come" (2 Corinthians 5:4–5). God works in you through His Word, your Baptism, and His Supper. He gave you His Spirit to keep the saving work Jesus did on the cross at the center of your life. No matter what happens or how you feel, God's Holy Spirit is working in you to complete His plan and to give you a perfect home in heaven.

Have you ever felt like no one loves you? Read John 3:16. God loved you enough to send His Son to die for you. Have you ever felt like you aren't pretty enough or smart enough or clever enough to keep up with your classmates? You aren't like anyone else. God made you special and different. And, through the saving work of His Son, He makes you perfect.

Pray: God, help me celebrate the plan You have for my life. When I put myself down, lift me up through the loving arms of Your Son. In His name. Amen.

RAPE

The scalding water hissed out of the shower-head and burned my body. But no matter how much I scrubbed, I felt like I would never be clean again.

Hot tears poured down my face as the horrible scene of my boyfriend raping me flashed in front of my eyes for what seemed the thousandth time. How could he have done that to me? How could he take something from me that, no matter how much I wanted to, I could never take back? My mind was whirling. Who could I turn to? What should I do? I began to pray. "Please, God, show me what to do."

God made me strong enough to tell my parents. They threw their arms around me in the longest group hug our family ever had. It was the first time I'd seen my dad cry. They got me the help I needed.

Read: Psalm 29:11

Three years later I still feel stabs of pain and betrayal when I look back on that day. The most difficult part is over. There is no more worry—Am I pregnant? Will I get AIDS? Should I tell my parents? What do I do when I see *him* again? What do I say to kids at school?

God answered my prayers that day. He gave me the strength to tell my parents. They helped me get the medical exam and the counseling help I needed. It took a long time to be able to accept myself again without shame, and to trust other people. I had been raped by someone whom I trusted, and whom I thought cared for me.

Looking back, I know God gave me strength that I never would have had on my own. My pastor told me that God sent His Son to die on the cross for me, to suffer in my place. Somehow Jesus felt my shame and anger and pain when He was on the cross. He rose again to win me a perfect, new life with Him. He has washed all my shame and sin away.

I can face things now without so much fear. I know God will always be with me. He brings me peace in the times I feel afraid.

Pray: Lord, thank You for giving me the strength to get through the hard times and for promising to stand by me through everything. In Jesus' name. Amen.

DEODORANT

Smells, odor, filth. We all suffer from body odor at one time or another. I'm not talking kiddy sweat; I'm talking grade-A, midsummer, sweat-on-the-back stench. The kind of smell that makes you gag just thinking about it. The aroma that may wash off in two showers—if you're lucky. We've all had it. We are humiliated if we smell that way on a date. Who wants to be with someone who stinks?

Where would we be without deodorant—all the sprays, sticks, and roll-ons—that save us from the embarrassment of smelling like a locker room? No one really ever thinks about deodorant while putting it on, but everyone knows when it's forgotten. Deodorant is designed to reduce, prevent, or cover up unpleasant body odors. That covering up and preventing sounds something like what Christ does with our sins before God our Father.

You might be thinking that comparing

Read: 2 Corinthians 2:15–16

Christ to deodorant is silly, but 2 Corinthians 2:15–16 says, "For we are to God the aroma of Christ among those who are being saved and those who are perishing. To the one we are the smell of death; to the other, the fragrance of life."

We are the aroma of Christ. What a great analogy! Have you ever stood outside after a rain in the spring and breathed in the wonderful aroma of God's magnificent creation? What a great feeling to know we carry with us, because of Christ's redeeming work on the cross and the Holy Spirit's empowering, the sweet smells of new life and the forgiveness of sins.

The next time you take a much-needed shower, remember the life-giving work Jesus did for us and the sweet smell of heaven He's won for us.

Pray: Dear Lord, thank You for giving us the fragrant aroma of forgiven children. Let us be Your aroma in the world, sharing the Good News of salvation in Jesus with all we meet. In His name. Amen.

MY SHEPHERD'S VOICE

I lay in the tent, too lazy to get up, listening to Kim clank around outside as she started the Coleman stove. It had been a miracle that our parents had let us go camping alone. The trip had been a blast so far.

We set up the tent under cherry and peach trees, full of ripe fruit. A river rushed by the campground, moving so fast that I'd had to grab Sam, my black lab, before he was carried downstream. We'd cooked hamburgers and toasted marshmallows, talking the whole time about our plans for college next year.

"Erin, come out here." Kim poked her head in the tent. Sam squeezed through beside her and landed on my chest. Laughing, I crawled out of the sleeping bag and pulled on my jeans.

"Look," Kim pointed when I came out of the tent. "There's a lamb running along the highway. Do you think we should try and catch it?" Sure enough, a lamb had somehow squeezed through the fence across

Read: John 10:2–16

the road and was running in confusion along the edge of the highway.

"He could get hit by a car," I said. "Let's get him and put him back inside the fence."

It's a good thing the colleges we had chosen didn't have entrance exams on sheep herding. The faster we ran, the faster the lamb ran. Sam, good little herder that he is, ran around the lamb barking crazily, frightening him even more.

We finally collapsed in laughter. At least the lamb was sticking close to the fence and not crossing the highway. Maybe he'd eventually find his way back in. Then a truck came barreling down the road, kicking up clouds of dust. We watched in horror, afraid the lamb would be so frightened that he'd run into the road.

To our amazement, the lamb stopped running and gazed at the truck. A man got out and lifted some sacks of feed from the back of the truck. The lamb ran to him as fast as its legs could go. Far across the field, the flock of sheep started moving toward the truck too.

Kim and I dissolved in laughter again. "It's the shepherd," I said. "The sheep know him!"

That night as we sat looking at the stars, I thought about my Shepherd. That lamb had been afraid to come near us, but he had no fear at all of the truck and the man who cared for him. I'd be leaving home in a few months, traveling to a new school full of strangers. It would be exciting, but frightening too. "Hold me in Your arms, Jesus," I whispered. "I need a good shepherd right now."

Pray: Jesus, Good Shepherd, guide me in the times of my life when I feel frightened and confused about what to do. Keep me safe in Your arms until it is time to live in heaven with You forever. Amen.

CARE TO TAKE A SPIN?

I remember the first day I got behind the wheel in driver's ed. I squinted into the bright sunshine, my hands clammy and my knees weak. I didn't know how I would make my body do what it was supposed to do. I turned the key in the ignition. The engine revved loudly. In my nervousness, I'd pushed my foot down on the accelerator instead of the brake. For the rest of the drive I was so upset about that single mistake that I had a hard time relaxing and paying attention to traffic. I must confess: I didn't drive well that first day.

Over the next few weeks my driving improved. But that one mistake still haunted me. Each time it was my turn to drive, I'd get really nervous and pray for the drive to be over quickly. I'd been practicing a lot, and without even realizing it, had become a much better driver. But my mistake was always in front of me, blinding me, holding me back from seeing what I had accomplished. My instructor encouraged me, never

Read: Jeremiah 31:34

criticized me, but even that didn't give me confidence.

I kept comparing myself to friends who never seemed to have a problem when they were driving. It became increasingly difficult for me to go to class. The day came to take our final road test. I knew that if I didn't pass this test, I'd never want to go through it again. I was careful and had a wonderful drive. When my instructor told me that I'd passed with flying colors, I collapsed in relief.

Looking back on that time, I realize that worrying over my mistake kept me from becoming the best driver that I could be. If I could have just concentrated on my driving instead of lingering on that mistake, I would have enjoyed myself.

It's easy to get into the habit of focusing on a mistake or something foolish that we did, even on a much bigger scale. We cling to our sin, letting it weigh us down, instead of bringing it before God and asking Him to forgive us.

My driving instructor encouraged me. Because of Jesus' sacrifice on the cross, God is ready and waiting to forgive us and help us live in His love. Jeremiah 31:34 says, "I will forgive their wickedness and will remember their sins no more." That's what God does—He forgives us for Jesus' sake, removing our sins, so that we can live as His children.

If a past mistake is creating a burden in your life, confess it to God now. He is ready to take the weight off your shoulders.

Pray: Dear God, help me to give You my burdens, and free me from guilt. Help me to know how much You love me. Let me enjoy living in the freedom of being Your child. Thank You, Lord. Amen.

CHOSEN WITH OTHERS

But you are a chosen people, a royal
priesthood, a holy nation, a people
belonging to God, that you may
declare the praises of Him who
called you out of darkness into
His wonderful light.

—1 Peter 2:9—

KELLY WARNEKE

WHO CAN SERVE?

I have a confession to make. I compare myself to other people. A lot! I look at them and think about how much better they are than me: they're better looking, are kinder, have more friends, are more intelligent, are more athletic, have more money, are more popular. . . . Sometimes I wonder why God allowed them to have lives that seem so much better than my own. Sometimes, I even begin to think that because I'm not as great as them, I can't serve God as effectively as they can. I look at other Christians who go to my church or my school, and I think, "God could never use me like He uses them. I'm not good enough for Him."

That's why I love the reading from 1 Corinthians so much. In it, Paul encourages his brothers (and sisters!) when they begin to think this way. Paul basically writes that God doesn't care about any of these "human standards" that we have. God doesn't look at things like our "noble birth" (which in today's world might mean being born into a rich or famous family), or how strong we are (either physically or mentally). Instead, God uses the "lowly things" and the "despised

Read: 1 Corinthians 1:26–30

things" for His glory. This might mean people who don't seem quite so popular or who don't have all the coolest things.

When someone is full of pride and thinks that they're "all that," because they're decked out with their iPod and their brand new car, or they are the best at everything they do, or they've just been named prom king, it can be kind of hard to serve God, because it seems like a reflection on their own power. Instead, God uses the lowly and despised things, "so that no one may boast before Him"—so that God's power is truly seen as God's power (1 Corinthians 1:29)! Whether you're the best student at your school or the worst, whether you're outgoing or quiet, whether you're super talented or don't like to stand out . . . God loves a humble heart, and will use you to serve Him!

Through Paul, God tells us that He has called us into the world, not because of anything that we've done or anything great about ourselves, but because of God and His mighty power! We don't need to worry about how much strength, or popularity, or intelligence, or talent, or wealth, or possessions we have. As you go about your life, always remember this comfort that you have—that God can and will use you to serve Him and His world no matter what you own or what abilities you have!

Pray: Dear Lord, thank You for the power and strength and ability that You have given me. Thank You for making me who I am and for working in my life, so that I can boast, not in myself, but in You. Please let me recognize that You have called me into the world, not by my own strength, but by Yours. Help me be encouraged and comforted by that, and let me always work to serve You and others by what You've given me. Lord, I pray this all in Jesus' name. Amen.

SWEET AND SOUR

The sweet taste of revenge or at least that is what it is called. It seems to be spreading like a wild-fire throughout our culture. Revenge is seen as a theme for movies, books, and practically anything else imaginable, including our lives. Take an eye for an eye, unless you can get both of their eyes while you are at it. I mean, if someone does something to you, you have the right to return the favor.

Though this is what the rest of the world is screaming at us, it is not what God says. He says, "Look, I know that you feel surrounded by evil, but when evil comes to you, temper it with good."

Let's take a serious look at revenge. How many times has it led to a friendship? Has it ever fixed the problem for good? I personally can only think of the negative outcomes in my life from my vengeance. It has spoiled friendships, ruined trusts, and destroyed chances at becoming friends with someone.

Read: Romans 12:21

"But not taking revenge makes you weak." Sure, some might say that it is weak to not take revenge. Those very same people could just as easily say that Jesus was weak on the cross when He asked His Father to forgive. But we know that is not the truth. In His act of willing submission, Jesus gained eternal life for us all. Through His suffering we inherit eternal life.

Though it is simpler and perhaps more enjoyable to take the "sweet" revenge, the effect always ends sour. Through His Word, God helps us to take the sourness of our lives and return the sweet message of the Gospel. May He help us to do so every day of our life.

Pray: Dear Jesus, thank You for taking the cost of my sins to the cross. Help me to live for You each and every day. In Your name I pray. Amen.

IT'S ALL IN HIS HANDS

As we mature into adults, so many things plague our minds. With choices to make and plans to figure out for the future, life can become very overwhelming. The age of responsibility has come upon us. More is expected of us, yet most of the time, we don't know what to do. We just go through life, trying to get by, while all the time we are worried and confused about our role in life.

Jeremiah 29:11 says, "'For I know the plans I have for you,' declares the LORD, 'plans to prosper you, and not to harm you, plans to give you hope and a future.'" How many times do we think that we have to hurry up and figure out our lives? How many times do we worry about the right college to go to, or what job to get? We all do that all the time. It gets overwhelming. Because we're only human, we can't figure things out by ourselves. But God tells us that He has everything figured out. Even with all

Read: Jeremiah 29:11–14; Matthew 6:24–27

of our anxiety about life, He has it taken care of. What's more, He has an amazing plan for each one of us. So instead of worrying about life and the future, we can let God take control and give everything to Him.

It's never easy. We become so used to relying on ourselves, but that's what makes us stressed. Let us instead trust God with our future. He has a beautiful plan for each one of us; one that we cannot even imagine.

While we wait for God to reveal His plan for us, we should remember that our timing is not the same as God's timing. Something that we want, or think should happen, may not happen at the time we think it should. It may not even be in God's plan for us. Yet we can always be sure that no matter what His plan for us may be, it is good. God is always faithful. He never changes.

So what risk is there in letting go of worry and stress? Let God slowly show you His big plan for your life. He will. He has your future in His hands.

Pray: Dear Lord, thank You so much for making a plan for me. In the midst of all that goes on, this is so comforting to know. I am so glad to know that I can trust You with everything, even the future. Help me to let go of the things that worry and overwhelm me, and remember that You are in control. Strengthen me through Your Word as I make decisions for the future, and help me to follow Your will. In Your name I pray. Amen.

SOUP OR SALAD?

As a tradition, my family always goes out to eat for each family member's birthday. I remember one particular dinner at the Olive Garden that turned out quite embarrassing. I told the waitress I wanted the Parmesan chicken meal. She in turn asked me if I would like soup or salad and waited for a response. I quizzically looked around the table at my family. Finally my brother leaned over and said "Ask her what the soup is." I looked up at the waitress and asked, "What's the super salad?" Then she gave me a curious look and said, "The soup of the day is . . ." Suddenly I understood what I had said. I could feel my face turning a deep red. My family found my mistake humorous and could not stop laughing. They had a reason to laugh . . . my blondness shone through.

Just imagine for a moment walking into a room full of people laughing. At first you think it is

Read: Luke 22:63–65; 23:35–37

CHRISTINE OBERDECK

great, what a happy place. But then you realize they are all laughing at you. You have no idea why. What did you do? Is there someone behind you they are laughing at? No, well then, why are they laughing?

It is not fun being laughed at. Jesus was laughed at too. When we think of Good Friday and Jesus' crucifixion, we commonly think of the physical torture Jesus suffered. But what about the hours before the crucifixion? Soldiers, kings, and others laughed and jeered at Jesus. They mocked Jesus and made fun of Him. Had He done anything to make others laugh? Had He mistaken the words "soup or salad" for "super salad"?

Although Jesus had the power to stop their laughter, He didn't. Out of love for you and me, Jesus suffered through the embarrassment and humiliation. Furthermore, He put on a crown of thorns, He was nailed to a cross, He died, and He rose from the dead. He is our Savior. Through faith in Jesus' death and resurrection we are set free from our burden of sin. We will live with Him forever because of His love and grace. We can rejoice in His love! Be happy—laugh—Jesus has saved us!

Pray: Dear Lord, thanks for being laughed at for my sake. You were humiliated, beaten, bruised, and crucified for me. Thank You for Your amazing love! Thank You that I can live each day rejoicing in Your grace. In Your precious name. Amen.

FIGHT THE GOOD FIGHT

"Do you guys mind if I get up and go to church tomorrow?"

That was all it took to send Melissa into gales of laughter. Everyone at our table looked at her as she announced, "Janelle's going to church tomorrow!" The table exploded with laughter and I was close to tears. One girl asked if I went to the Church of the Black Savior, a church for Satan worshipers.

I ran to my room in tears. I hadn't cried since the night before I left for Dartmouth. I was a junior in high school, going to a debate workshop at the New Hampshire college. My parents had prayed with me that night when I was so nervous about leaving home for the first time. I remember thinking the prayer was pretty stupid. What was God going to do, stand beside me and hold my hand? Now I realized how important those prayers really were.

 Read: 2 Timothy 4:7

That week my roommates had bugged me every night when I read my devotions. On Friday night I read a devotion called "Steer Your Peers." I knew my time to stand up as a Christian had come. But trying it in the cafeteria the next morning had left me confused and hurt, unable to understand why my friends would persecute me for believing in Jesus.

I called my parents and they offered advice and prayers. I wasn't sure then which I needed more. Sunday morning I went quietly to church. Everyone there was so kind that I almost cried again. These strangers were more my friends than my campus-mates because we shared a common Lord.

A few days later I received two letters from friends at home saying they had prayed for me that Sunday. My youth pastor sent me a card and wrote on it, "I have fought the good fight, I have finished the race. I have kept the faith" (2 Timothy 4:7).

I came home from Dartmouth a different person. I know now that nothing's too tough for me and God, armed with His Word and a lot of prayers. I'm not afraid to speak up for Christ anymore.

Go ahead. Take a stand. Fight the fight with Jesus at your side.

Pray: Father in heaven, give me the courage to stand up for Christ. Remind me that You hold me in the palm of Your hand and will help me in every situation. Amen.

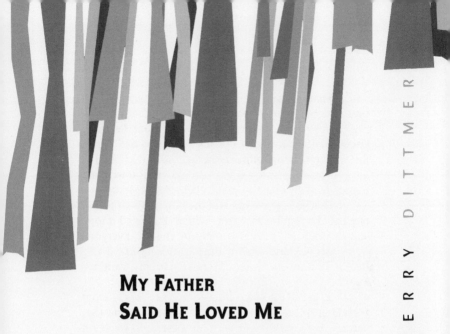

TERRY DITTMER

MY FATHER
SAID HE LOVED ME

Last night my dad finally said he loved me. I wonder why it's so hard for him.

It was a rather ordinary evening. We were just sitting at the kitchen table. I was working on some homework, and Dad was paying some bills. We weren't really saying much of anything to each other.

Most of the time when we do talk it's the regular teen-parent kind of stuff. You know. Dad says, "I don't want you doing that." Or he says, "I'd better not catch you doing such and such." Or, "Back when I was your age, blah, blah, blah." And I mostly just say "yeah" or grunt something back.

It's not that we don't like each other. My dad's okay, all things considered. And I think he basically respects my space. We just don't talk about it much.

 Read: Psalm 127

So it was kind of weird last night. He and I, sitting there, kind of aware of each other. Suddenly he just up and says, "I love you, Son." It was amazing. It really was. It felt so good to hear him say it. It felt so good to hear the words. It was really wonderful.

And then I did something I don't do very often. I said, "I love you too, Dad." Last night makes me wonder though. If it feels so good to hear it, why don't we say it more often?

Pray: Thank You for Your love, and thank You for my father. Help me to love him and not be so stingy in showing it. In Jesus' name. Amen.

FRIENDS

Margaret and I have been best friends since the first day of first grade. Growing up, we were inseparable. I can't see her picture or say her name without recalling some silly stunt we pulled, like the time I accidentally gave her a black eye! Now we live a thousand miles apart, but we still burst into laughter over nothing when we talk. The phone company could use us for a commercial. Margaret seems to know my thoughts better than I do. We've always been there for each other, no matter how many miles separated us.

The closeness Margaret and I share is no accident. We developed our trust and friendship over a long period of time. I thank God that He gave me a friend to share in joyful times and in troubled times. Maybe you have a friend like Margaret, whose smile makes you laugh and whose shoulder is there for you to lean on.

 Read: Proverbs 18:24

God talks about close friends when He says, "There is a friend who sticks closer than a brother" (Proverbs 18:24). Just how close is "close"? According to Jesus, the ultimate demonstration of love for a friend is the laying down of your own life. We might have to think twice about giving our lives for a friend. Jesus didn't. He gave His life, not only for those who cared for Him, but for those who made fun of Him and rejected Him too.

Jesus' example models friendship for us. He shows us how to love at all times—not just when we're in the mood or a friend is treating us right. He shows us how to love when our best friend makes team captain and we don't. Friendship centered in Christ rises above everyday problems and soars to heights of understanding and love.

Friendship can be a risk. When you become friends with people, you give a piece of your life to them, and they to you. You develop a lifetime of memories—some that are pleasant, and perhaps some that you'd just as soon forget. Jesus gave much more than a piece of His life. He lovingly gave up His whole life to win you forgiveness and salvation.

The next time you are with a close friend, before you start laughing and joking around, tell that friend that you thank God for your close friendship. Go ahead. Take the risk.

Pray: Lord, thank You for placing good friends in my life. Forgive me when I take them for granted and forget to let them know what they mean to me. Thank You for being my best friend and for giving Your life for me. Amen.

JOHANNA BELDON

I'll Never Speak to Her Again!

Have you ever held a grudge? I have. Grudges seem to be a part of life. Jack gets mad at Jill for what she said to him, how she looked at him, or what she told his best friend about him. Suddenly he is holding a grudge. If you've ever held a grudge, you know it isn't easy. We grudge-holders must at all costs avoid any *civil* conversation with that person. We can't be seen with her friends; and whenever there's a gossip session, we've got to throw in a list of her latest crimes. After a while this list gets harder to maintain, but we keep telling ourselves we've got to keep it up.

For all this hard work we only hurt ourselves. We tend to be easily irritated and unhappy because of the bitterness inside. Keeping up with the gossip gets complicated, and messing up a story can mean

Read: Matthew 18:21–22

losing even more friends. We usually end up with less than what we started with.

So how do we get around the old grudge? One word—forgiveness. Thank the Lord, God didn't hold a grudge against us. If He had, we would all be doomed to hell. But He didn't do that, He forgave us. One of the best ways we can thank Him for that is to forgive others when they sin against us.

Pray: O Lord, forgive me for the grudges and grievances I bear. Where my relationship with another is strained or broken, guide me to reconciliation. Help us forgive each other, for Jesus' sake. Amen.

REBECCA DIFATTA

ARE YOU LIKE YOUR SISTER?

My sister got straight *A*s all the way through grade school. She didn't even really have to try. She could study five or ten minutes and ace a test. Through high school she continued to be a straight-*A* student as well as being in the National Honor Society. She was the yearbook editor and co-valedictorian, with her best friend at her side achieving the same honor. She was never seen without a thesaurus in her back pocket, and she was a major player in the drama club.

Now in her third year of college, taking eighteen credits a semester, my sister is still an absolute overachiever. I, on the other hand, am a normal student who makes average grades and participates in just a few activities that I enjoy.

It's very hard at times to live in the shadow

Read: Leviticus 19:18

of my sister's reputation for excellence. Every teacher I meet remembers my sister and expects me to perform at her level. Even my parents sometimes expect the same from me, and no matter how I try, I just can't live up to the standard of achievement set by my sister in our family.

As I've grown older, I've been able to talk to my parents about the fact that my brother and I don't have the ability to be great students and excel at all kinds of activities as well. It's been hard on all of us, but we are learning that none of us can be a carbon copy of someone else.

God gives each of us special gifts. We have the responsibility to use them to the best of our abilities to glorify Him. Not all of us can be like our neighbors or relatives. But that doesn't mean that we're out of the game plan of life.

God expects from us only what He knows we can do and nothing more. He doesn't call us to be like our neighbors, only to love them. In fact, He tells us to love our neighbors as we love ourselves.

I sometimes envy my sister, but I know God loves me the way I am. He doesn't want me to be like anyone else. He chose me for His child and gave His Son to be my Savior. I'm not exactly like my sister. And that's fine.

Pray: Lord, help me to understand myself and like myself. Remind me, when I compare myself to others, that You love me the way I am. In Jesus' name. Amen.

THREE IS A CROWD

Cindy and Kelly were inseparable. A casual observer would have trouble telling if Cindy lived at her own house or at Kelly's. They even spent time together doing drills at basketball practice. Then Kelly's grades dropped, and her parents told her she couldn't play basketball anymore until she improved them.

Cindy still went over to Kelly's house every day, but during basketball practice she met a new friend—Cary. Cindy invited Cary to go to Kelly's house with her. They hadn't really noticed Cary before, but now they found they had a lot in common, and soon there were three friends.

After a while Cindy felt that Kelly and Cary were becoming so close that she was being pushed out. It was not fair. After all, she had helped them get to know each other. Cindy confronted Kelly and Kelly said she understood and was sorry. But things

Read: 1 John 4:7–12

didn't really change. Cindy began to doubt herself. Had she done something wrong, or did Kelly just not like her anymore?

There are many different endings to this story, not all happy, some sad. When we are realistic about relationships, we know that at times we will feel jealous, at times we will be left out, at times we will long for new friends.

In those times it is good to remember the friend who will never leave us, who is never preoccupied with anyone else.

God is always willing to listen to our happy news, and our problems as well. Go to Him in prayer, listen to the advice He gives in His Word, and trust Him to help you work things out. He is always working for your benefit.

Cindy and Kelly grew distant in their relationship. That will happen from time to time with earthly friends, but never with God. He loved you enough to give up the life of His Son for you, and He will always love and care for you.

Pray: Dear Lord, give me patience and understanding in my relationships with my friends. When things don't go right, guide me and show me Your plans for me. In Jesus' name. Amen.

JENNY HARRIS

On Loan

How do you deal with the death of someone you love? I grappled with that when my cousin died. I didn't know what to do or where to turn for help. I thought that Kevin went into the hospital for appendicitis. The next thing I knew, my aunt called to tell us that he had died. When an autopsy was done, we learned Kevin had had acute leukemia. He was only fifteen.

For a while after his death, I felt angry with God. I didn't understand why He had taken away someone we loved. But I realized that God also loved Kevin. Then I remembered what my aunt had said, "I guess God only lets us borrow them for a while."

I thought about this for a long time and realized how true it is. We all are God's children. For a time He puts us into other people's lives to help, understand, and love. But finally we go to our true home.

Read: Revelation 21:4

Not that God wanted people to die. Death is the result of sin in the world. But through the death and resurrection of His Son, Jesus, God has defeated sin. He takes us home, where we all truly belong, with Him in heaven.

We on earth may mourn, balancing our hurt with remembrances of a special person, but we thank God for the home to which that person has gone.

Pray: Dear Lord, creator of life, please help us to understand Your love and to find hope when we lose people we love. Please give us strength in our time of mourning and joy in the promise of heaven. In Jesus' name. Amen.

PROM NIGHT PROMISE

It's that one special night of high school, prom night. For some it's the biggest experience of their teenage years. It's also the night on which more girls get pregnant than in six months of Friday nights combined.

Tonight Chad and Julie will enjoy dinner, dancing, and a feeling of being grown-up. But the highlight of their evening will not be wrestling in the backseat of Chad's car, or making it on the beach, or being at some party where the kids are so high they don't even remember who they came with. Julie and Chad will spend the evening walking along the beach, not rolling in the sand; taking a moonlit drive, not driving the upholstery. As Christians they will honor God's expectations for them.

God tells us not to abuse our bodies sexually. Our bodies belong to God, not to us, because He

Read: 1 Corinthians 6:18–20

made them and redeemed them with the blood of His Son, Jesus.

Backseat promiscuity is not God's idea of a great date. This doesn't mean Christian teens spend every date playing checkers and telling knock-knock jokes. Still we want to honor God and live as He wills. And He promises us the power to do just that.

More important, we have His promise of forgiveness when we fall. He goes with us on the first date, to prom night, to the altar, and beyond.

Pray: Lord, help me to stay away from sin and sinful situations. Give me strength to choose friends and dates that will help me to honor You with my body. Thanks for Your promises! Amen.

 (RICH BIMLER)

"I LIKE SEX!"

Maybe you feel uncomfortable with those words. But God's Word tells us that He created male and female, as sexual beings, to be gifts for each other. And that is good!

The problem is that sex has been turned into something altogether different from what God intended it to be. Magazines, movies, television, the Internet, and other media portray sex in negative ways. Sex is used to sell cars, deodorant, jeans, and beer. Sex has become a way to use and control people.

One problem these days is that too many people want to open these gifts at the wrong time. People are encouraged to give in to their sexual urges. Some people are so preoccupied with sex that it has become addictive—like doing drugs. Sex can hold tremendous power over us.

What do God's people do? First, we affirm sex as a gift from the Lord; we rejoice that He has

Read: Genesis 1:27–31

made us male and female. We also affirm God's design—a monogamous relationship between one man and one woman for life. Then we can help each other talk through our questions, fears, concerns, and struggles. And we can go to our Lord when we mess up, giving thanks for His forgiveness.

Sex is a gift, a wonderful gift from God. I like sex!

Pray: Lord, thanks for the gift of my sexuality. Help me to celebrate this gift and to use it wisely. When I fail in my relationships with others, reassure me with Your strong forgiveness and set me back on track. Thank You for making me as I am. Amen.

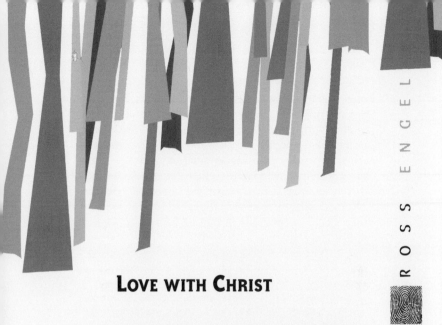

LOVE WITH CHRIST

I started dating a girl at the end of my senior year of high school. At that time I thought she was "the one." We spent a lot of time together doing the things most teenagers do on dates, each of us believing that we would be together forever.

However, something was missing in our relationship. My girlfriend had been baptized, but she only had been to church a half dozen times in her life, mostly for weddings and baptisms. She did not really know much about Christ and His great love for us, or what faith is. She did not know God and was set on not bringing Him into our relationship.

As a Christian, this placed a great strain on me. Getting my girlfriend to come to church with me often meant I had to bribe her. I would buy her gifts to make her happy. It seemed like a worthwhile sacrifice because she was going to church and maybe was learning about the love of God. Gifts

Read: 1 John 4:7–12

were not the answer, though; her heart was not open to Christ. Every opportunity I took to talk to her about my faith was met with indifference and a closed mind and heart.

A relationship without Christ at the center is difficult. As young adults, many temptations come into a relationship. Overcoming these temptations can be done only with the strength Christ gives. Most important, sharing the same faith and the love of Christ strengthens a relationship.

True love is a gift from God. It was displayed when He created human life in a perfect world, demonstrated again when He sent Jesus to die for us (1 John 4:9), and is seen every day as we build relationships with family members and with others, even in dating situations. Christ demonstrated His love for us so we can share love with others.

Put God and His love into your relationships. His love will strengthen the love you share and can make it last. Find someone with whom you feel comfortable talking about Christ, someone who will share your faith in Christ. The relationship will grow and be strong with the help of God! Remember, love and relationships are gifts from God.

Pray: Heavenly Father, thank You for the gift of relationships. Help me always to place Christ at the center of my relationships. Let them grow with Your love as the center, and help me always to remember that relationships and the love shared between people are something You designed. In Jesus' name. Amen.

KNOWING GOD IS ALWAYS WITH YOU

It had been an absolutely horrible day for Scott. It all started when a blurry vision of his mother appeared above his face at 6:15 a.m. As his eyes opened from a peaceful slumber, his mother's irate face pressed down toward his with the lovely greeting, "You over-slept! Get up. Now!" Looking at the clock, the reality of the situation dawned on Scott, and he hurriedly threw back the covers and stumbled out of bed.

Scott made it to school just before the late bell. He hadn't had a chance to brush his unruly hair, and his friends and homeroom teacher stared strangely at him when he entered the classroom. Scott told himself that things could only get better. Unfortunately, they didn't.

During first period—algebra, a class he was hav-ing trouble with—Scott got back a test for which he had

Read: Psalm 16:8

studied extremely hard. Scott sat silently while the tests were handed out, hoping he had at lest gotten a C. The ugly red F stared up at him from the paper, as if taunting him.

At his locker, looking in his mirror and trying to fix his hair, Scott heard his girlfriend's voice. Sighing with relief that he could have a talk with her, Scott turned to speak to her. The sight that met his eyes caused his mouth to drop open and his eyes to bulge. His girlfriend, Sarah, was kissing some guy from his science class! Overcome with emotion, Scott slammed his locker shut and ran all the way to his next class.

Every teen has a day like Scott's. It seems as though nothing turns out right and everyone is against us. During one of these frustrating days, have you asked God for help or thought about opening the Bible? Do you wonder if God is with you through these times or if He cares what happens to you? The answer lies in Psalm 16:8. Saying this verse to yourself in times of turmoil can give you peace in the midst of a troubled day.

God sent His Son, Jesus Christ, to walk the way with us, especially in the middle of a terrible day. Christ knows what we face because He faced it too. He brings us hope and strength when we need it most. Knowing that God is always with you is something that can get you through anything.

Pray: Heavenly Father, let me always remember that when I have a problem, You are always with me. No problem is too great for me to face and conquer because You are by my side. Through Jesus Christ, my Savior. Amen.

JUDGING OTHERS

Finally! Camp is here, and I'm totally pumped for this upcoming week. I look around and see nothing but familiar faces. Then, I see her. With her blonde hair, perfect body, and nice clothes, I can't help but envy her. We weren't really enemies or friends last year (or so I thought), but I had been sure that she was truly a snob. She had been in my cabin last year, but I hadn't really gotten to know her.

At dinner, I found that she was in our group to go rock climbing and rappelling. I didn't know it at the time, but God had a wonderful plan in store that involved both of us. When we went rock climbing and rappelling, we discovered that we had a friend in common, and we hung out. At first I was uncomfortable because I didn't know whether she was judging me, but I figured, *I'm at camp, and I should just be myself.* So I was.

Later that night, she sat with me and some

Read: James 3:13–18

other friends for dinner. It was awesome to see God at work! Within the few hours that we spent together, a friendship had formed. As the week went on, we got to know each other better, and I let go of the envy and jealousy that had made me perceive her as an enemy. Instead, I had gained a friend.

As I look back on that week, I realize Christ gives us the power to go beyond our sin and seek forgiveness and reconciliation. My envy and sinful pride almost destroyed the opportunity for friendship.

God's Word reminds us that envy is a sin. It separates us from God. However, we can ask forgiveness for the times we envy others and trust that because of Christ's death God does forgive us. And He will help us to see the good in others and become peacemakers. God will work in all things for our good—including showing us friends where we thought we had enemies.

Pray: Heavenly Father, I'm sorry for the times I envy others. Thank You that through Jesus' death, all my sins are forgiven. Help me not to prejudge, but instead to look at the unique gifts You have given to those around me. Thank You for the unexpected ways You bring friends into my life. In Jesus' name. Amen.

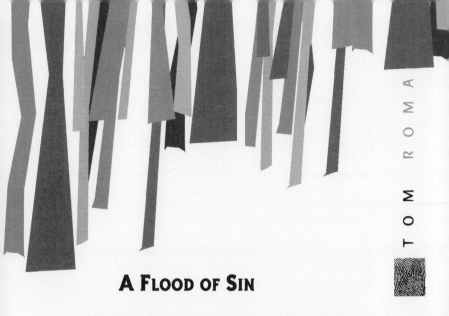

A FLOOD OF SIN

One day as I left for school, it was a wonderful sunny morning outside, but not for long. The sky darkened, the sun hid in the overwhelming clouds, and it began to rain. It started raining and didn't stop for days. (This would be the start of the worst flooding in Missouri history.) Later in the week, the creeks and rivers around our house began to break over their banks. It continued to rain. We were actually sandbagging around the doors and windows to keep water from coming into the homes.

After an especially bad rain, I noticed that the sewers in the streets were filling and overflowing into neighbors' yards and driveways. As I came into my house, my heart sank. We had been working so hard on the outside that we hadn't noticed that the house was filled with water. It smelled horrible. The sewer had backed up. Our basement had

Read: Psalm 119:105–112

almost two feet of sewer water in it—gross!

After about five hours of moving everything, trying to salvage all the items that had not been touched, the rain stopped. As the water receded, we found stains, dirt, and muck everywhere. Many valuable things had to be thrown out because of the contaminated water and the odor. The whole family was upset.

What an example of what sin does to our lives and our families. This was a real-life illustration for me about the contamination of sin. Sin comes into every home and touches every family. It reaches into everyone's life. Sin consumes everything vulnerable.

It wasn't until clean water power-flushed out the contaminated sewer that we could start rebuilding our basement. God can clean up the sin in our lives. The Holy Spirit works through the "power-cleaning" of our Baptism. By God's Word and Sacraments, we are made new.

Ask God to open your eyes and heart to the needs of those He has placed in your life. As you see those needs, pray for an opportunity to present the life-changing words and work of Jesus Christ. Only He can meet your deepest needs, clean you "to the foundation," and bring refreshing forgiveness.

Pray: Dear heavenly Father, forgive my sin and wash me clean in the love of Your Son, Jesus. Open my eyes and heart to Your mercy and Your saving grace every day. Let me share Your power with others so we may be closer to You. Through Christ, my Lord. Amen.

PARENTS

"Mom, are you wearing that?!" Lauren asked as they were leaving for dinner. The outfit wasn't that bad . . . for the mom on *The Brady Bunch!* Lauren, on the other hand, was wearing something stylish.

I guess we have all had those days when one of our parents pulls out those bell-bottom pants or sings "Yakety Yak" to us. And it's really embarrassing, I know. I have two parents who still haven't gotten the fact that we are living in the twenty-first century. We need to understand that they probably went through the same things with their parents. It's because we are from different generations. Your mom may like her polyester pants while you prefer your jeans. These things are easy to deal with; it can't be *that* bad to adjust to different style preferences. It's like accepting different personalities at church and school.

 Read: Proverbs 17:6

But how about priorities, morals, that kind of stuff? I'm sure you have disagreements on "teen issues." My parents used to be big on the dating topic. Was fifteen too young? Should I wait until I am thirty? Or how about your choice of friends? Do your parents ask you about their families and lifestyles?

It may seem annoying, but you need to accept that they have been through it all. They aren't brain-dead. They love you and care about you. Listen to their advice and be patient with them. They are only concerned about you. Can you imagine what it would be like if your parents didn't give a rip about where you go and whom you date? We really do need them. A lot of things have changed over the years, but many of the problems we go through now were there twenty years ago. So they understand.

Our parents' styles may be different and their opinions may be opposite ours, but we are all here now, together. We are all children of God. No matter how diverse we are, we have that in common—God loves us and gave His Son to die for us. That *never* changes.

Pray: Father, thank You for the gift of parents. Help me to listen to my parents and to respect them even when I disagree with them or when they embarrass me. In Jesus' name. Amen.

SUICIDE

Jill seemed to have a perfect life. She was popular, drove a great car, had great parents, and basically got along with everyone. The whole school was shocked one Sunday night when Jill tried to kill herself.

As strange as this may sound, it happens more often than we'd like to think. I've read results of a national survey that state that about twenty-four percent of teenage girls consider suicide in a given year. Many of these people attempt suicide and some complete their suicide attempts. (Guys also attempt suicide.) These people feel over-whelmed by life. They think that life is meaningless, that they aren't pretty enough, nobody loves them, or that they never do anything right. God doesn't think so! He has plans for all people (see Jeremiah 29:11–13).

If you know anyone who is feeling this way,

Read: Jeremiah 29:11–13

try to help him or her. Tell her how much she means to you. Tell him how much he means to God. Help her to get some counseling. Who knows? One day you could be so hurt that you feel that life isn't worth living. It is! God gives us a chance. He isn't finished with us yet! God can and will help us, all of us, in rough times. He loves us so much He gave His Son for our sins and raises us to life through faith.

Pray: Dear Lord, remind me that You have plans for me. Keep showing me that my life is not a waste. I know my reward will be great in heaven. Help me stick out the pain and keep my faith in You. In Jesus' name. Amen.

MIND YOUR OWN BUSINESS

"What do you think about the way Cassandra and Marcus are acting?"

All I had to say was, "It's none of my business." However, I chose to make it my business. So I said, "I think it's awful. And you know what, I bet . . ." Then I proceeded to tell everyone what I thought was going on between Cassandra and Marcus.

After we had that conversation, I didn't feel guilty about talking behind my friends' backs. We were just talking like we always did. In fact, I forgot all about the conversation until the phone rang two nights later. It was Cassandra.

It seems someone had told Cassandra about the conversation. Cassandra wanted to know if I had said those things. I told her the truth and then she told me the real story. Boy, did I feel stupid! I apologized and Cassandra forgave me, but our

Read: Proverbs 16:28

friendship would never be the same.

We weren't "just talking" that day. We were gossiping. Not only did it hurt Cassandra and Marcus, it hurt us too. Because Cassandra found out her "friends" were gossiping about her, she would never trust us in the same way again. Gossip hurts people— even destroys them—and it doesn't show love. But Jesus died for us all and loves us all—even the people we hurt with our gossip.

Now, whenever I feel the urge to gossip, I just remember how close Cassandra and I once were, and I feel sad that we're not that close anymore. Basically, I think of what the consequences could be if I don't mind my own business. And I remember what Jesus did on the cross—for me, for Cassandra, for everyone.

Pray: God, thank You for blessing me in so many ways, especially through all my friends. Help me to treat my friends just like Jesus, our best Friend, treats us. In Your name. Amen.

CHOSEN TO THE WORLD

"*You are My witnesses*," *declares the Lord, "and my servant whom I have chosen, so that you may know and believe Me and understand that I am He. Before Me no god was formed, nor will there be one after Me.*"

—*Isaiah 43:10*—

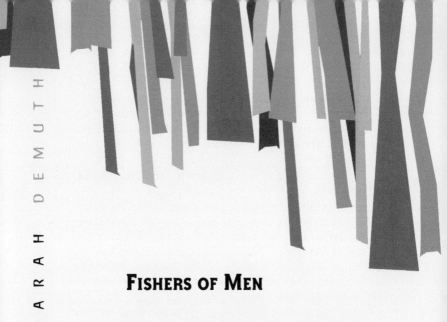

FISHERS OF MEN

Have you ever considered yourself a "fisher of men"? Did it feel like God was calling you specifically to work as one of His workers? I've had that feeling on two separate occasions.

After the last National Youth Gathering, our pastors decided that instead of going on a trip every three years, we would participate in various servant events every year. The spot we decided to go to the first year was upstate Idaho. Truthfully, I didn't sign up to go on this trip with a servant's heart, I signed up to go because I like to travel and I have never been to Idaho before. Our service included setting up camp where we were staying. During that time, we got to know the other campers. To me, it was just like any other camp I have gone to.

Every night we gathered for worship—it was then that I heard God's call for me. It was like He brought me there for a reason, so that I could learn

Read: Matthew 4:17; 28:19

more about Him and tell others about being His followers. He chose all of us to be there to spread His kingdom and His glory. When we got home, I told my friends about my experience, and how being there opened my eyes to the many ways we can serve God.

Last year, our youth group went to Angola, New York, and helped out around the community. We were split into small groups to go out and help different families. We had opportunities to tell these families about our faith. It was a moving experience for me. It felt like God was using me again, and saying, "Come, follow Me, . . . and I will make you fishers of men" (Matthew 4:19). God used His Word to make me understand Him better.

God works in His own way with everyone. You never know when He will use you to tell others about Himself. He is always pointing us in the right direction, saying, "Go and make disciples of all nations" (Matthew 28:19). God's Spirit helps us draw strength from His Word and Sacraments and learn to follow our Lord's will. God has chosen us to the world and invites us to gather as fishers of men.

Pray: Heavenly Father, help us to hear Your voice when You call us. You have chosen us to be fishers of men, which is not the easiest task to follow. We do not always feel comfortable talking with our friends about You. Strengthen our faith so that we are able to talk about You to others, so that they may be Your chosen ones too. Open our eyes to see Your people in need and equip us to meet that need. In the name of Jesus Christ our Lord. Amen.

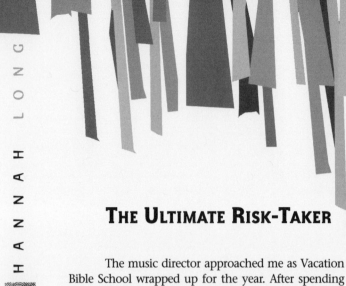

HANNAH LONG

THE ULTIMATE RISK-TAKER

The music director approached me as Vacation Bible School wrapped up for the year. After spending the past five grueling days belting out the repetitive songs of the program, I was somewhat tired. She advanced closer, and I awaited what she would say. Expecting something akin to, "Nice job this week!" or "Did you have fun working the music station this summer?" I was reasonably surprised when she asked me something different. "Hannah, would you consider directing the children's choir this year? I really think you'd be the right person."

I never would have expected to hear anything like that! Me? A teenager? Direct the children's choir? I was only a few years older than some of these kids! Surely there was someone else better equipped or older that could lead. Why pick me? What did I know?

Fear does crazy things to us. Deep down I loved the possibility of directing the children's choir, but to be completely honest, I was scared. Based on what I know about some of my talents, I agreed with our

Read: Jeremiah 1:7–8

music director: I could do the job. But in the back of my mind were those ever-present, nagging doubts. I doubted that God might really want me to do this, and I doubted that I was gifted enough for such a task. I was too afraid to trust God and take the risk.

There's an old saying that goes, "God does not call the qualified; He qualifies the called." What exactly does that mean? It means that you and I have been called, individually and personally, by God Himself. It means that He has chosen you and me for the work of His kingdom. It means that whatever our age, wherever we are in our Christian walk, God is asking us to go out on a limb and trust Him, because He will give you the ability to accomplish what He calls you to do.

Had I reacted out of fear, I would have missed the many incredible opportunities to test, strengthen, and renew my faith that God provided through this adventure. There have been times when I struggled and stumbled a bit, but God is faithful and He led me through despite my initial fears.

Being a Christian is a risky business. You have to risk being different, being rejected, being picked on, being unpopular, and being lonely. Who in their right mind would willingly chance these things? You and I do it every day. Why? Because One greater than you and I already did. Jesus lived the life of the ultimate risk-taker. He said things, went places, and hung out with people who didn't benefit His social life. He risked it all (and gave it all too) for you, me, and the entire world. He loves us more than we'll ever imagine; we have no reason to fear.

Pray: Dearest Jesus, forgive me for the times I've reacted out of fear and neglected to trust You. Grant me a spirit that is willing to take a risk when You call me to do so. Thank You for being the ultimate risk-taker, taking my place and my sin so that I can be with You forever. In Your name I pray. Amen.

THE LORD'S SERVICE

One cold and bitter night, a young soldier was walking through the streets of a city when he saw an old beggar man shivering next to the road. With little thought for himself, the young soldier had compassion upon the man. The young man unsheathed his sword and cut his own cloak, wrapping the old beggar in half of it. Later that night, the young man had a dream about what he had done. But, rather than the old man, Jesus was the one wrapped in the cloak.

This story—the legend of Saint Martin—shows that, although we do not realize it, when we serve others, we are truly serving Christ. Although we don't see Christ directly in those we serve, as Martin did, He is still there. The Lord Himself even addressed the issue of service in His Word. "The King will reply, 'I tell you the truth, whatever you have done for the least of these brothers of Mine,

Read: Matthew 25:31–40

you did for Me'" Matthew 25:40.

This Scripture helps remind us that even the most menial tasks, such as doing the dishes, or washing clothes, or painting the fence are works of love in response for what Christ did for us on Calvary. "Whatever" includes not just the big things but the little things also. Christ works through us no matter the circumstances. As chosen children of Christ, we can remember that our service to others is a service to Christ Himself.

Pray: Dear Lord, help me to serve You joyfully and to dedicate every act as a service of love to You. Thank You for the ultimate act of love, the gift of Your Son as my Savior. In His name I pray. Amen.

YOU FEED THEM

Some of my teachers love giving tests; they just make me nervous. Pop quizzes are even worse. But did you realize that even Jesus gave "pop quizzes" to His disciples? In John 6 Jesus and His disciples were surrounded by 5000 hungry men, plus women and children. Jesus asks Philip, "Where shall we buy bread for these people to eat?" (John 6:5). John adds that Jesus asks this question only to test him, for Jesus already had in mind what He was going to do.

Sometimes it seems like Jesus asks us to do something that we cannot do. In Luke's account of the feeding of the 5000 Jesus tells His disciples, "You give them something to eat" (Luke 9:13). Now there's an impossible test to pass! With Philip we would respond, "Eight months' wages would not buy enough bread for each one to have a bite" (John 6:7) or "Are you talking to me, God?"

Like the disciples we see the physical needs

 Read: John 6:1–13

of those around us. They may need food, shelter, or other basics of daily life. But what they need most of all is the same thing that crowd needed—they need a Savior. Jesus' disciples didn't understand that His direction that they should feed the people wasn't referring to just their physical need for food, but also to their spiritual need for salvation. Through the power of God's Spirit at Pentecost, the disciples were equipped to carry out the work of feeding the hungry souls throughout the world.

You and I get to participate in that task. God gives us His Word and Sacraments and strengthens us to share the news of Jesus with others. In all that you do you have the opportunity to share God's message of salvation with others. What do we have to offer Jesus in the way of resources? Probably just 5 loaves and 2 fish. But when we put what we have in His hands, it will be more than enough . . . and there will be leftovers.

Pray: Heavenly Father, sometimes the task before me looks impossible. Strengthen me. In faith let me trust in You. Help me to be ready and willing to share Your Word when the opportunity arrives. In Jesus' name. Amen.

A RELUCTANT SERVANT

Last spring break my parents signed me up to go with our church youth group on a mission trip to Mexico for five days. I already had plans to hang out with my friends all break. I was really mad when my parents told me I had no choice but to go. Besides the fact that I wouldn't know anyone, I hated the thought of being stuck in a foreign country doing nothing but building houses and feeding dirty homeless people. I was thinking about running away to a friend's house until the bus left, but that was a little childish. Already ten minutes late, I packed a bag of clothes and left for church.

I was surprised to discover that after the first day in Mexico I was having so much fun. It turns out I knew one girl on the trip who went to my elementary school. We were pretty close the whole trip. I met lots of other people too. Seven of us spent three days helping build a house for a large family.

Read: Luke 7:11–17

It felt really good knowing I had done something that would actually make a difference in someone's life. But the thing that touched me the most was when we all went to an orphanage. I visited with kids ages 3 to 12. All of them were so thankful to God that He had given them the life they had. They were so happy with the little they had and the "fiesta food" they had (which was not a lot). To them it was a huge amount of food. I felt really sad when this blond-haired, blue-eyed boy came up to me and asked me (in Spanish) if I was his mother. (I have blonde hair and blue eyes too!)

I thought my trip to Mexico was going to be horrible, but in the end, it turned out completely the opposite. God used this experience to help me grow up and appreciate the things I have. I'm glad He did.

The story of the widow's son (Luke 7:11–15) reminds us of Jesus' compassion for a woman He did not know. He saw the despair of the woman and, without being asked, brought her dead son back to life. Deserved or undeserved, asked for or ignored, Jesus came to live and die for us, to show His love to all. Through Him we receive faith, forgiveness, and eternal life.

Pray: Heavenly Father, just as through Christ You showed Your mercy to the widow and her son, help us to share Your mercy with others. Use us to carry out Your work in our world. In Jesus' name. Amen.

WHY, GOD?

"Pelham got shot."

Until my friend told me that, it had been just another cold winter day with nothing to do. I've known Pelham since I was four. He's been like a brother to me, since he and my older brother have always been best friends. Pelham always looked out for me because I was the youngest.

We called Pelham "The Preacher." We all knew God and loved Him, but Pelham would constantly *do* for the Lord. One day, when Pelham saw an old man cold and shivering with no coat, he gave him his jacket. He didn't even mind giving his jacket away. He said, "The Lord will give back to me."

Pelham's always putting money in the offering at church. And he takes food to people in the neighborhood—even a lady we all know is a prostitute, because he knew she was hungry and didn't

Read: Matthew 25:40

have anything to eat.

When I heard that Pelham had been shot, I couldn't help asking God why He let it happen. Pelham never did anything to anyone, except try to be a friend.

Pelham survived. He is out of the hospital and doing the things he used to do. I guess I was wrong to question God's authority when I thought Pelham would die. I know we can't earn God's favor by doing good things. And I know God didn't cause Pelham to get shot. Jesus gave His own life for Pelham and for me, and for all the people in the neighborhood. He says when we help someone else, we are really helping Him. I think that's why Pelham does it.

One day Jesus will thank us for giving Him food when He was hungry and a drink when He was thirsty. He'll say, "I tell you the truth, whatever you did for one of the least of these brothers of Mine, you did for Me" (Matthew 25:40).

That will happen on the Last Day when Jesus takes us to heaven. I'll be there. I think Pelham will be too.

Pray: Lord, sometimes I question Your authority. Remind me, even in times of sorrow, that You are ready to help in every situation. Use me to share Your love with everyone who needs my help and Yours. Amen.

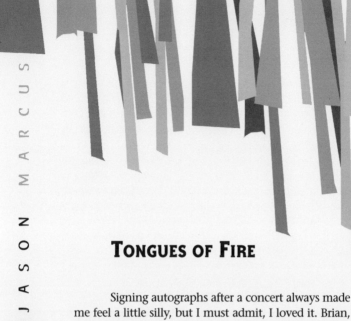

TONGUES OF FIRE

Signing autographs after a concert always made me feel a little silly, but I must admit, I loved it. Brian, Kirk, and I had started our Christian rock band, Tongues of Fire, during our junior year in high school. We sang at different churches, parties, and sometimes for relatively big concerts in our area. We were starting to get nice reviews in the local papers, mentioning "fresh rhythms" and "engaging style." None of us were bigheaded enough to think we were on our way to a recording career, but our performing helped us save money for college.

A man's hand stretched out of the gloom into the bright circle cast by the light over the stage door. "Will you autograph my program, please?" I dissolved in laughter. It was Pastor Avanti. He laughed too. "I'd like to talk to you, Jason. Do you have time for a midnight snack?" I said sure, and ran back to the dressing room to tell Bri and Kirk I was leaving.

Pastor and I drove to a Mexican restaurant

Read: Romans 12:6–8

down the street. We ordered nachos and leaned back to talk. "Jason, you have marvelous musical talent. And when you gave your testimony tonight, it sounded natural and confident. I could sense the Spirit moving through your words, touching people in the audience. The woman next to me was crying. Your words about Jesus' sacrifice on the cross obviously helped her in a very real way.

I sipped my Coke and looked away, embarrassed and not sure what to say. "Jason," Pastor went on, "have you thought about becoming a pastor?" He laughed as I used my napkin to wipe up the Coke that I'd jolted out of the glass when I jumped in shock.

"A pastor? I . . . I don't know. No one in my family has ever . . ."

Pastor didn't let me finish. "I don't mean to lay a burden on you, Jason, only a suggestion," he said. "You are gifted in the way you speak and sing. You seem to have an honest desire to tell people the Good News that Jesus is our Savior."

I'd never thought about it before. It had always seemed like the group had just been something fun to do, something that could earn us some money in a fun, sometimes even exciting way. But I did look forward to giving my testimony, to talking with the adults and kids when we sang, and to telling them how much Jesus loved them.

It was a suggestion, Pastor said. Maybe it was a calling. From God Himself. I'd definitely listen.

Pray: Dear Lord, show me how to serve You in whatever profession I choose. Let me use the skills and talents You have given me to share the Good News that Christ died and rose again with everyone around me. In Jesus' name. Amen.

DAVID

The dance was full of happy people, smiling and laughing. Everyone was having a great time. Everyone, that is, except David.

"Hey, David," I greeted him enthusiastically. Then I realized something was wrong. "Are you okay?"

"Yeah, I'm fine." But he sobbed and turned away in embarrassment. "I'm sorry," he said. "I just don't want to talk about it." And then the problem came out—"It's not my fault that my parents hate each other."

Poor David! I spent the rest of the night talking with him. Coming from a close family it was difficult for me to understand what he was going through. I began to realize the terrible pain of seeing two people you love so much constantly at each other's throats.

When I got home that night, I began thinking that there was only so much I could do to comfort David. I began to search through my Bible to find a

Read: 1 John 3:1

passage that would bring David a message of comfort from God. I decided to share 1 John 3:1 with him. "How great is the love the Father has lavished on us, that we should be called children of God! And that is what we are!"

As David and I talked about this verse, we realized how great it is to have God Himself as our Father. Not only are we heirs of His kingdom, but we receive His protection, comfort, and solace in our troubles. We took David's concerns to God in prayer. We knew God listened and promised to help David.

Because we live in a sinful world, earthly families sometimes experience difficulties and even fall apart. It's painful to listen to parents disagree. It's torture to hear slamming doors and angry words. When you hear it, it may feel like your world is being torn away from you. All your security is vanishing.

Thank God, His family cannot fall apart! When our earthly families have troubles, God calms the waters with His Word and love and forgiveness, shared with us in His family Supper.

When your family relationships are troubled, read God's Word and receive His comfort and strength. Pray for healing and solace from the sadness. Talk to your pastor and ask for his advice. God, your Father, holds you in the palm of His hand. He forgives the sin of broken relationships and heals the pain of broken homes.

Pray: Dear Father, heal the brokenness in Your children's homes. Use me to share Your love and comfort with those who need it. Please help with all the Davids of the world and their families. In Jesus' name. Amen.

KATHLEEN JOZA

DON'T LET ANYONE
LOOK DOWN ON YOU

Cockroaches scuttled down the dim hall as I knocked on the door. A child, maybe eight years old, opened the door a crack. She carried a baby wearing only a diaper. I caught a glimpse of smaller children running wildly around the room and a woman, lying in a drunken stupor on the couch. "We're having a show," I told the kids. "Would you like to come?"

Loud music blasting from a speaker filled the neighborhood and attracted children to the run-down camp where we had set up our show. I was on a mission trip with kids from my church, helping share Jesus' love in the South Carolina projects. In this poverty-stricken area, children came willingly when we knocked on their doors offering free entertainment.

We took turns speaking into a microphone,

Read: 1 Timothy 4:12

giving our testimonies about Christ's work in our lives. We performed puppet shows and dramas and dances, all expressing God's love to children who didn't get much love at home.

I held a little girl on my lap and told her about Jesus. She listened intently. I knew she didn't get this kind of attention at home. In her eyes, as I told her that Jesus loved her enough to give His life for her, I was Jesus. I knew I was making a big impact, I pray a saving impact, on this little girl's life.

I realized at that moment that just because I'm young doesn't mean that I don't fit into God's plan or that I have to wait a few years to start serving Him. And I don't have to travel far away on a special mission to start serving Him either. God gives me, and you, plenty of opportunities to serve Him right now. He may help you share His love with a lonely neighbor, a hurting friend, or a family member who needs to know Jesus.

St. Paul told his young helper Timothy, "Don't let anyone look down on you because you are young, but set an example for the believers in speech, in life, in love, in faith and in purity" (1 Timothy 4:12). I remember again that precious little girl that I held in my arms. Maybe the Holy Spirit worked through my words to bring her to faith in Jesus. It didn't matter that I was only a teenager. I was the one who picked up that child that day. Now when I remember her small face, I whisper, "Thank You, God. Thank You."

Pray: God, please show me opportunities to serve You and others. Help me remember that each day is a gift from You to use in Your service. Thank You for Your never-ending love. In Jesus' name I pray. Amen.

Take This Job—
And Give Thanks for It

It was a typical day at work. Long lines. Numerous balloon orders. A woman throwing a fit because she was in a hurry. I looked at my watch—two hours to go. I hate this job, I thought to myself. I just want to go home.

If you're like me, you have probably held some sort of a job to save money for college or to earn extra spending money. I started working at a Hallmark shop a year ago to save enough money to buy a car for college next year.

If you've been on a job search, you know that it isn't easy to find one. I was rejected at several places. My self-esteem got pretty low—it seemed as if no one wanted to hire me and I would never find a job. Finally a job opened up and I started to work.

I realized that God had opened a door when I

Read: 1 Thessalonians 5:16–18

least expected. Even though I know God helped me get my job, I really don't enjoy it, and I wish I didn't have to go to work. A lot of people feel that way about their job from time to time. Jesus certainly understands that experience. He asked God, if it were possible, to let Him turn down the job of going to the cross for our sins. But even in that job, He followed God's will. His suffering earned our salvation.

1 Thessalonians 5:16–18 says something to me about my attitude at work: "Be joyful always; pray continually; give thanks in all circumstances, for this is God's will for you in Christ Jesus."

Does Paul mean that I should really say, "Thank You, God. I love hearing this woman scream at me to hurry, and the way her kid is crying makes me feel very joyful"? I don't think so. But God is giving me the opportunity to earn money, and I thank Him for that.

My job is not forever. I thank God for that too. I'll continue to work and ask God's help to find another job I can enjoy. I can thank God for the lessons I've learned in this experience too. I've learned that I don't want to be in the retail business as my future career. I've learned how to be a servant to people who need help, and a good steward with my money.

All of my discomfort will be worth it when I have the satisfaction of buying my own car with my hard-earned money. That's something to be joyful about!

Pray: Dear Lord, help me learn from opportunities that aren't exactly joyful. Help me to be grateful for all that I can learn in the experiences You give me. In Jesus' name. Amen.

CELEBRATION

I grabbed Nate's arm before he could send his bulletin-airplane sailing over the balcony rail. Glancing down, I saw Pastor Jeff staring in horror under the pews. Kiesha and Darrel were crawling through peoples' legs up to the altar where the kids from our youth group were presenting the Good Friday chancel drama we had written.

Good Friday? Black Friday. Our week as Servants for Christ at the central-city Cincinnati church had been thrilling up until now. Six of us had traveled together from our church in Nebraska. Pastor Jeff had greeted us with the words, "You can help me plan the greatest Easter celebration we've ever had."

Hank, the church janitor, had moved out of his room in the parish hall so Lacey, Liz, and I could stay there. Pastor Jeff pointed out that the room had been rat-proofed—the holes in the walls had been

Read: 1 Corinthians 15:56–57

filled with plaster. Tim, Chad, and A. J. were staying with members of the church down the street.

The week flew by. Hank took us to an Alcoholics Anonymous meeting. He stood up and said that he had spent time in jail for theft and had lived in an alcoholic stupor until Pastor Jeff had talked to him about Jesus. Now he worked at the church and hadn't had a drink in six months. He praised God for the new life God had given him.

We went with Pastor Jeff to make calls. We learned to yell before we went down an alley, sending all the rats scurrying to hiding places. We entered dark, dilapidated apartment buildings with overflowing trash cans sitting in the hallways. Pastor invited everyone to come to the church and get to know us, and to be sure and come to our Easter celebration.

We invited every kid we saw to come over to the church every evening for games, music, and stories about Jesus. By Wednesday night we had 75 children thrilled at the thought of singing as a choir on Good Friday and Easter. Lacey and Tim and I presented puppet shows about Jesus, while Liz and A. J. and Chad played pool with the older kids and led Bible study. Over and over we told the kids, Jesus loves you. He loves you so much, He gave His life for you. Then He rose again so that you can live with Him in heaven.

Good Friday. Our week exploded in disaster. Pastor Jeff was so disappointed in the kids' behavior in church that he left without talking to us. That night we heard a gunshot in the street. In the morning Chad told us that one of the kids who had been coming to Bible study had been shot. He might not live. Pastor Jeff came and told us about Hank. He had been arrested, drunk.

Easter morning dawned and we gathered early

in the church. We felt no excitement, only relief that the week was over. Then the kids started arriving, faces shining and many of them wearing new clothes. Their families filled the church. The kids sat like angels, then stood to belt out "Jesus Christ Is Risen Today." We couldn't stop grinning. God did work miracles, and the greatest one was raising His Son from the dead for us, and for these kids.

Pastor Jeff had tears in his eyes as we climbed into our van to start home. "We did it," he said. "We had our Easter celebration."

Pray: Jesus, let me shine with Your love wherever I am. When it seems like I'm failing, remind me that it is You who works through me to accomplish Your will. Amen.

CHANGE

Change—what a big impact it can have on a person's life. I sure had a big change in my life. My dad is a pastor, and one November he received a call to a church in California. At the time, my family and I were living in Nevada. We belonged to a wonderful growing congregation, and we kept busy with school, sports, and music. I had just started high school. I, for one, did not want to move.

The night that I was hit with the news that my dad had accepted the call, I cried myself to sleep thinking life was not fair. The move would mean a huge change in my life and in the lives of others.

The following March my dad moved to California, leaving the family behind to finish the school year. The next few months were hard on the rest of us as we prepared to leave Nevada. In June, we joined my dad in California to start our new life.

That fall I had to start at a new high school

Read: Hebrews 13:7–8

and meet new friends. But I made the volleyball team and started attending youth group at my church. Some of the girls at my church helped me out by showing me around school and by being my friends. In October, my family moved into a brand-new house. I had my own room. All those changes began to look much more positive.

Hebrews 13:8 tells us, "Jesus Christ is the same yesterday and today and forever." No matter what changes occur in our lives, Jesus Christ will not change. He always will be our Savior. His love and compassion can overcome any doubt that we have. He will remain faithful to His Word.

I have now lived in California for more than a year, and I really enjoy it. Jesus has been with me every step of the way. When changes occur in our life, remember that the one thing that won't change is Jesus Christ and His saving love that He gives to all who believe.

Consider these questions the next time you face change in your life:

- Why does God allow change in our lives?
- Can good things come out of change?
- What reassurance does the Bible give to us about change?
- What change for the world occurred when Jesus died for our sins?

Pray: Dear God, thank You for Your never-changing love. Thank You for Your Word and the hope that it gives to me. Please help me through the tough changes, and help me always keep my focus on You. In Jesus' name. Amen.

DONINE FINK

WHERE'S YOUR TREASURE?

My youth group participated in a servant event in Little Rock, Arkansas. Our project was to paint and do light yard work for elderly people. When my group reached our first house, we realized that we had our work cut out for us: The yard was an absolute jungle, the paint thick and dirty on the brick house. Our group got right in there, busily chipping the paint and cleaning the porch. By the end of the day, it appeared we hadn't made much progress.

We talked to other groups who said they were almost done with their first house. Then I realized that the best we could do was to make this house look livable. Before the trip I had envisioned making the houses look new and classy. I had a mistaken idea of what beauty was and how the house should look.

Although we couldn't give the owner of the

Read: Matthew 6:19–21

house an elegant home, we could give this woman something she wanted and needed. On the last day of work, I left a card that had a personalized version of John 3:16 on it. She may never have fame or wealth, but she could be offered an even greater gift—the great gift of the Gospel. Jesus died and rose for her!

In Matthew 6:19–21, Jesus reminds us of what is really important. All worldly goods and advantages are meaningless. Even all the hard work done to that house will surely rot again, but the gift given to us through Jesus' death and resurrection will never pass away. God would have us look toward our heavenly goal with Christ, our priceless treasure, leading us there.

Even if you feel unable to help someone in any other way, what does Jesus always want us to share with others?

Pray: Dear God, in this sinful world, help me to focus on storing up treasures in heaven. Help me to share the Gospel so others can enjoy the treasures of heaven also. In the name of Jesus Christ, my Lord. Amen.

THE RESCUERS

Abortion has become a remedy for ignorance and irresponsibility. For many people, abortion has become a way to preserve the economic, emotional, and social integrity of all parties involved. They feel that a "quiet" abortion is a better alternative than bringing a child into the world. They are blinded by their own selfishness so they cannot see that their relief is pain for the child they are killing. As a result of these selfish acts of irresponsibility, millions of children will be killed.

We scorn cultures where barbaric acts of genocide are being carried out. We fight to save those dying of hunger and AIDS in Africa, and we send troops to Bosnia and Kosovo to save innocent people who are victims of social injustice. We speak out against concentration camps and gas chambers, yet we allow millions of American children to be savagely slaughtered. Accountability and responsibility

 Read: Proverbs 24:11–12

should never be overshadowed by trends or pop culture. When we allow ourselves to succumb to those ideas, our integrity no longer has any validity.

As Christians, we have been given new lives in Christ, and we can strive to protect those on the verge of becoming victims of abortion. We can approach this tender issue with hearts full of the compassion and forgiveness Christ has demonstrated toward us. And we can educate those "staggering toward slaughter" about how precious the gift of life really is. In Deuteronomy 30:19–20, God reminds us about the importance He places on life: "Now choose life, so that you and your children may live and that you may love the LORD your God, and listen to His voice, and hold fast to Him. For the LORD is your life."

Just as the Spirit of God pleads on our behalf, we have a responsibility to "speak up" for the helpless. From newborn cries to tottering first steps, we can celebrate that life truly is precious in God's eyes. With the light of Christ illuminating our lives, let us witness with the courage and conviction about the gift of life. Consider these questions about the sanctity of life:

- What measures can we take to encourage those considering abortion to seek a different solution?

- How can we be witnesses to others about the sanctity of life?

Pray: Dear God, illuminate my heart with the light of Your love as I witness to others about the gift of life. Thank You for sending Your Son to rescue and save all the children of the world. In Your Son's name. Amen.

HE HAS PLANS FOR YOU

Once there was a baby abandoned in a far-away country. She was left to die in the town's garbage dump. But while this infant was dying of hunger and rats nibbled on her bare skin, by the grace of God, a nurse happened to walk past. Seeing this poor child so close to death, the nurse brought the baby to the local orphanage.

Meanwhile, in another country, a family was moved by God to adopt a child. They were blessed to receive that abandoned baby—rat bites and all. God had a special place for this child. The family raised the little girl in the church, and she grew in stature and in faith to be an amazing woman of God.

Today, you can find this woman doing missionary work in Guatemala, raising her own family, and spreading God's Word. This wonderful lady is my aunt. When I think about how her life began

Read: Jeremiah 1:5

and where she is now, I can't help but be proud. Being related to such an awesome lady has truly inspired me.

God had a very special place for each one of us. And even though God's call to you may not necessarily be foreign ministry, it doesn't have to be. You can be a witness for Him anywhere you go or in whatever He wants you to do. Whether God wants you to be a Sunday School teacher or a repairperson, there always are opportunities to shine your Gospel light.

I love telling that story about my aunt. It shows that God works miracles in our lives, even when we may see the situation as hopeless. God gave us Jesus, who died on the cross to show the greatest love that ever existed. In Christ we have the gift of forgiveness and eternal life. He gives us faith to be His witness and to proclaim His amazing grace. God sees potential and promise in each one of us. We were created to do His will.

The Lord will fulfill His purpose for me (Psalm 138:8).

Pray: Dear heavenly Father, please help me realize that You have plans for me. Help me to live for You and to touch the lives of others through my words and actions. I want to be Your instrument; use me as You planned. In Jesus' name. Amen.

JOSHUA DEHNKE

I Was Hungry

Hmmm . . . I like fettuccini Alfredo . . . but I haven't had manicotti in ages, . . . and linguine sounds delicious, I thought, studying the menu at my favorite Italian restaurant. With so many choices, how could I decide?

Suddenly, a different thought popped into my head: What if I had *no* choices and finished dinner still famished?

I like to eat. My friends will attest to that. My parents could show a long supermarket receipt as proof. Sometimes complete strangers ask me how I can eat so much. I tell them I have a very fast metabolism or that I'm just a growing boy. Leftovers? Not in our house. Seconds? Of course. Full? Not likely.

However, on this particular evening I thought about how many others would go to bed on an empty stomach—in my hometown of St. Louis, in America, or in the world!

 Read: Matthew 25:35–40

How often do I actually think about world hunger, and, when I do, how real is it to me? After all, *those* people live miles away, and I only see them on television. I do not give to the hungry, but does it matter? Feeding one person for one meal is insignificant.

Jesus disagrees: "I was hungry and you gave Me something to eat. . . . I tell you the truth, whatever you did for one of the least of these brothers of Mine, you did for Me" (Matthew 25:35–40).

It doesn't matter who or how many I could feed, or how much I could feed them. When I feed the hungry in any small way, it is service to the Lord. Through my offerings at church, helping with food drives, or praying for the hungry, I can do something small to help with a big problem.

Pray: Lord Jesus, help me to see the pains of those around me and throughout the world. Remind me of Your unconditional love that caused You to give Your life, even for me. Help me to share that love with all I can touch, near and far. In Your name. Amen.

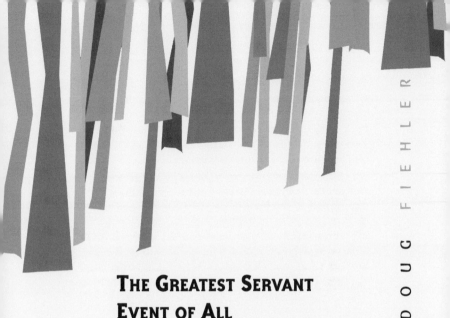

DOUG FIEHLER

THE GREATEST SERVANT EVENT OF ALL

One Christmas morning a little boy began opening his presents. He ripped off the wrapping paper, peered inside, gave it a little attention, then ripped into the next present. To him it was Christmastime, a time to receive presents and enjoy them.

He thought that the stack of presents would never run out. The pile grew smaller and smaller with each opened present. He was very happy . . . until he looked up and saw no more presents.

The tears welled up in his eyes and he began sobbing. He threw a tantrum and laid there moaning on the carpet. His mother picked him and up on the sofa next to her and said, "I was so happy to be giving you all of these presents, and you were happy to receive them. Then when you ran out, you

Read: 1 Corinthians 6:20

became upset. Son, it is more blessed to give than to receive."

Two thousand years ago we were given the greatest gift of all. Jesus Christ came to relieve us of the burden of our sins. He showed His love to all people. This was the greatest servant event of all.

As the son in the story, we were enjoying all of the gifts our Father had given us, but not all in the way they were intended because of our sinful nature. He came, saved us, and showed us His ceaseless love.

He also commanded us to "go and make disciples of all nations" (Matthew 28:19). He wants us to spread His Word and love to all people. What better way to do this than by serving others.

Pray: Lord, thank You for the greatest servant event of all time. Help me to be a servant to others and to You. In Jesus' name. Amen.

TOOLS OF THE TRADE

On the first morning of the servant event, I sat in the cafeteria after breakfast where about a hundred other ready-to-work youth anxiously awaited deployment to our work sites. In the doorway a stocky middle-aged man stood. He introduced himself as Greg, the person in charge of the work projects. Greg remained standing in the doorway with a basketball under his right arm and a hammer in his belt. Standing there, silent in his denim overalls, Greg had a very blunt way of presenting himself. We listened as if waiting for a speech or special presentation.

Finally Greg asked, "Any basketball players in the room?" A few people hesitantly raised their hands. Greg chose a volunteer, Angie, and tossed the basketball to her as he continued, "This is the most important tool you may use all week."

I looked around the room, noticing heads

Read: Matthew 22:40

turning with inquiring looks. Greg went on to say, "God created each of us differently. These differences should not hinder a person but should help a person to achieve goals and to accomplish tasks. People have different strengths, and only those who see differences as limitations manage to limit their abilities.

"Jesus said He came into the world to serve, not to be served. He served by willingly paying for our sins on the cross. Because of His service, there are many ways we can serve one another. Some of us can pound a nail into a piece of wood, others can help someone with a jump shot. You will be a servant and a witness to God this week. If it is not through pounding a nail, then it may be through spending time with a child in the neighborhood or helping an elderly person cross the street."

How will you serve God today?

Pray: Father in heaven, grant me the strength to be of service to You in all that I do. Help me to walk in Your ways with the tools You have given me. On this day I am very proud to have been called. I ask this in Jesus' name. Amen.

ANOTHER CHRISTIAN CHAMELEON

"Good morning, Mr. Peterson!"

"Good morning, Cindy. How was your week?"

"Just fine. Oh, hi Jake! How's the knee? I've been praying for you."

"Thanks, Cindy, it feels better. The doctor says I should be off my crutches by the end of the week."

"That's great to hear. See ya."

It's just an average Sunday for Cindy. First she greets people before church starts. Then she goes to worship. After worship she helps with Sunday School classes. Finally she tops the morning off by hanging out with kids her age from her church at a local restaurant.

She is a fun person to have around, and her

Read: 2 Corinthians 6:14–18

friends appreciate her Christian attitude toward life. But she isn't always this way.

"Hey, Cindy! Are you coming to the party tonight to get drunk?"

"Wouldn't miss it for the world."

This is another average ritual for Cindy. Only this time it's Friday night. After work Cindy usually gets invited to a party. She knows that there are going to be a lot of things there she shouldn't mess with such as getting drunk, doing drugs, and possibly sex, but she usually goes anyway.

After she's under the influence of not only chemicals but the people who are there, she starts saying and doing things she usually wouldn't say or do.

Then she's back to Sunday morning:

"Good morning, Mrs. Tillmen!"

"Good morning, Cindy. How was your week?"

"Just great! Hey, Julie, it sure is good to see you here at church. How's it going?"

After less than 48 hours she seems like a totally different person. Some might call her a hypocrite.

What kind of environment do you surround yourself with? And how does it affect the way you act? Think about it.

Pray: Father God, thank You for being an awesome God. Lord, grant me wisdom so I may make the right decision about the people I surround myself with. Forgive me for Jesus' sake for all the times I have not made decisions as I should. Remind me to turn to You for the strength to do what I know is right. Amen.

MAKING NOISE

My friend and I, both involved in musical groups at school, were asked to share our love of music with the first- through third-grade classes at our church. We were a little wary at first but were soon delighted to sing with them. There was one girl in class who had a special impact on me. She was normally quiet, but when she sang, it was with all her might. Most little kids have fairly decent voices, missing a few pitches occasionally. This girl, however, never hit the right note. She would sing louder than any of the other kids, sometimes getting strange looks, but she sang with a smile on her face. She seemed like an angel in a heavenly choir.

Why was this little girl so different from the rest? She sang from her heart. That's what God calls us to do: praise Him with whatever talents we have. He doesn't want us competing with one another for the position of best singer or most talented baseball

Read: Psalm 33

player. God doesn't care how many people we beat. He cares that we praise Him in all things. The little girl loved the Lord so much that it didn't matter if she couldn't sing a note. The Bible says to make a *joyful* noise to the Lord, not a beautiful one. And we have so much to praise God for. After all, He loved us so much, He died for us and made us clean. That's certainly reason to sing!

So whatever talents you have—music, theater, art, sports, or even mathematics—praise God fully with them. He loves to see His children praising Him with all their hearts. It's not hard to praise God after all the wonderful things He's done for us.

Pray: Lord, help me today to praise You fully with whatever I do. You've done so much for me that sometimes I get carried away with my talents and turn them into a competition. Help me to get over my competitive spirit and focus on glorifying Your name. Amen.

SCRIPTURE INDEX

DEVOTION: _____ **PAGE:** _____

NOTES

DEVOTION: PAGE:

NOTES

NOTES

NOTES

DEVOTION: _____ **PAGE:** _____

NOTES

NOTES

DEVOTION: **PAGE:**

NOTES

NOTES